THE 52nd FLOOR

WHAT PEOPLE ARE SAYING ABOUT THE 52ND FLOOR

'*Thinking Deeply About Leadership*' is a perfect subtitle for this book. Why? Because as you read and get actively involved with the process which Levy, Parco, and Blass created for the reader, you will think deeply about what leadership means to you. This book on leadership is all about you and your leadership point of view, not about the authors' and their leadership point of view. Wow! What a great learning opportunity.

Ken Blanchard
Author of *The One Minute Manager*

❋

Leadership is certainly a subject that requires deep thinking because it determines success or failure in every human endeavor. *The 52nd Floor* is a non-traditonal approach that provides the reader with a unique glimpse into leadership. A must read for those serious about developing as effective leaders.

Bill Looney
General (ret.), USAF

❋

It takes courage and imagination to write such a book. I can only hope that more will follow. I like the way the questions have been posed, how myths have been shattered, and the emphasis on thinking deeply rather than repeating trivialities. Very well done.

Amnon Rapoport, Ph.D.
Distinguished Professor of Management
University of California–Riverside

❋

Whether in the locker room or the board room, on the field or in the office, leaders constantly influence behavior. This book is ideal for anyone who has ever wondered about what it means to lead. Levy, Parco, and Blass, have given us much to think about – their book is a winner!

Coach Bobby Bowden
College Football Hall of Fame

❋

An absolutely fascinating look into leadership. Levy, Parco and Blass have fully grasped a picture and spectrum of leadership that has taken me a lifetime to discern. This book will make you think.

Michael J.C. Roth
President Emeritus
USAA Investment Management Co.

❋

Bravo! The authors have written a brilliant and wholly unique leadership book. The inclusiveness and participatory nature of the book will inspire anyone who is interested in management. Once you get started, you won't be able to put it down.

Robert N. Mishev
McKinsey & Co.

The 52ⁿᵈ Floor provides an extraordinarily fresh and mentally stimulating look at the development of great leadership skills. This book will challenge many old business school paradigms and will stretch your imagination. It offers wonderful insight into new vistas of effective leadership. Combining theory, practical experience and exciting new science, *The 52ⁿᵈ Floor* takes you on a journey into what great leadership will look like in the future. This is a home run!

E. Lee Rice D.O.
Chief Executive Officer
Lifewellness Institute

❀

Over the years, I've learned that people at every level of experience and responsibility learn about leadership best from stories which resonate with their own life. The stories in this book are engaging in themselves, but even more importantly they cohere so that taken together the stories become a powerful and useful perspective on good leadership practice. The book's a gem!

Rich Hughes, Ph.D.
Senior author of *Leadership: Enhancing the Lessons of Experience*

❀

I read *The 52ⁿᵈ Floor* and I think these authors have a winner on their hands. This book has the power to transform emerging leaders today into more thoughtful, ethical leaders in the future. It's a must read for anyone looking around at how the world has changed in the last six months and looking to grow as stronger leaders in the future. The creative writing style is reminiscent of another favorite book of mine, *The Goal.*

Patrick Murphy
Senior Vice-President
ING

❀

Finally, a leadership book that will actually improve one's leadership! *The 52ⁿᵈ Floor* sees leadership as a journey, a practice of what real people do in real time to create practical value right now. Here is a natural and realistic direction that we can take to make our leadership journeys successful.

James R. Barker, Ph.D.
Editor, *Management Communication Quarterly*

❀

Most of the entries in the perpetual parade of leadership books have, in some way, shape, or form, tried to explain what is, and who will be, a good leader. Conspicuously and refreshingly different is Levy, Parco, and Blass's new book. *The 52ⁿᵈ Floor* implies that leadership represents the artistic brushstrokes framed by the contextual canvas. Transmitted quite interestingly through anecdote, story, and metaphor, *The 52ⁿᵈ Floor* is a breath of fresh air in an otherwise rather stale leadership literature.

Gerald R. Ferris and Pamela L. Perrewé
Authors of *Political Skill at Work: Impact on Work Effectiveness*

❀

The authors take readers on a powerful journey of critical thinking exercises that builds tools for successful decision making. Every chapter of this book offers metaphors for leaders that pull away the crutches that too many people have been relying on. I would recommend *The 52ⁿᵈ Floor* for leaders of leaders who want to increase the adaptive capacity of their organization.

Kerry Plemmons
Clinical Professor, Institute for Leadership and Organizational Behavior
University of Denver

I found *The 52ⁿᵈ Floor* to be provocative and challenging while at once elegant in it's simplicity. Take a scenario and think deeply about the leadership implications! It sounds simple, but the drill-down exercise allows the reader to go deeper and deeper into the "so what" of the equation on a level rarely achieved by other authors. As a Chief of Police in Evans, Colorado, I am using their book and concepts in developing leaders within my organization. Their book is already a well-worn addition to my library!

Rick Brandt
Supervisory Institute

❋

When I lead large change efforts, I like to tell the organization's leadership that in order to enact their current change initiative, they need to put a sticky note on their bathroom mirror that reads, "*What am I doing for change today?*" Then they need to read that sticky note every morning, everyday, while they brush their teeth, for about the next five years. It looks like Dave, Jim, and Fred have created the perfect sticky note.

Ken Stoltman
DRS Technologies, Inc.

❋

This book really made me sit back and reflect on my leadership style and on those that work with and around me. There will be many that will learn from your work (I did) and become better leaders if they apply some of your lessons.

Randy Spetman
Director of Athletics
Florida State University

❋

The book is a very good read – and different. I've read many leadership books. *The 52ⁿᵈ Floor* profoundly changes the discussion in a way that practical leaders can relate.

Ronald A. Poussard
Senior Executive Service

❋

A wonderfully refreshing book that provokes thinking, reflection and the insight needed to design a meaningful, creative, leadership path.

Frank J. Prochaska, Ph.D.
Author of *Metamind: Think and Lead*

❋

If you are serious about leadership, *The 52ⁿᵈ Floor* deserves your time. Don't rush the reading. Savor the experience.

Linda Hillmer
Chief Executive Officer and President
CorpComm Inc.

❋

For those who truly care about leading well, there is always a struggle to find the balance within ourselves. How do I communicate effectively and with ease? How do I encourage the best in those around me and also deliver the best in myself? How do I deal with my own self-doubt? What Levy, Parco and Blass achieve here is to make this journey deeply insightful and also fun. It's a must read for those who embrace the challenge to lead in today's world.

Dan Oates
Chief, Aurora Police Department, Colorado

The difference between ordinary and extraordinary leaders is a refined ability to see deep within themselves and those they lead. Any leader who is committed to life-long learning simply has to read this book – it is unlike any other.

Wendy Wallace
McKinsey & Co.

❀

Compelling, practical, and straight-to-the-point real world stories that challenge leaders to ask the right – and tough – questions. A must read in these challenging times when leadership matters most!

Keith Kennedy
Chief Investment Officer
General Electric Healthcare Financial Services

❀

At times, I hated reading some of the stories in this book because they forced me to acknowledge that many of the faults I might see in others are largely those I try to ignore within myself. That said, I absolutely love this book and believe if people read it, they will discover it to be an immensely powerful tool.

Nathan Atherley
Silicon Valley, California

❀

As I began my journey into *The 52nd Floor*, I was immediately struck by the preface and the following: *"Great leaders are those who have a refined ability to adapt to change"* and *"Increasing your adaptive capacity is what we aim to do with this book."*

Fantastic! Life really is about change and our response to it. Change is a constant, but our response is not. Leaders responses are dynamic and morphing constantly. There are no Newtonian Laws commensurate with our response to change. Therefore, in my mind, success is tied to those possessing the awareness of self in response to the dynamics of change. This is precisely why the study of leadership will never end. It is a study more of self than rules, checklists, catch phrases, etc.

Quite frankly, this book has been a tremendously enlightening read. I have not read a book on "leadership" that turns the focus primarily onto the leader by way of introspection! The unique methodology and approach to leadership have been refreshing and truly useful.

Calvin Ball
Washington DC

❀

At times, I hated reading some of the stories in this book because they forced me to acknowledge that many of the faults I might see in others are largely those I try to ignore within myself. That said, I absolutely love this book and believe if people read it, they will discover it to be an immensely powerful tool.

Nathan Atherley
Silicon Valley, California

❀

As an MBA with military experience, I thought I knew all there was to know about leadership...until I read *The 52nd Floor*. The book's fresh approach captures the reader's interest because the book is about everyone's favorite topic – ourselves. Through memorable stories and insightful questions, *The 52nd Floor* asks you to question your assumptions, identify your barriers, and build your ability to cope with change. Today's leader cannot afford to be mediocre. If you just want to look like you know what you're doing, skip this book and follow the latest trend. However, if you truly want to better your organization and better yourself, this book is essential. I plan on rereading this work several times. Once you begin your journey with *The 52nd Floor*, you will see why.

Mike "Quatto" Posey
Virginia Beach, Virginia

David A. Levy   James E. Parco   Fred R. Blass

The 52nd Floor
Thinking Deeply About Leadership

○

ENSO BOOKS

United States of America

Published in Montgomery, Alabama by Enso Books LLC.

Control illustration by Pamela Parco, p. 154. (2008)
Bongard puzzle images originally drawn by Harry Foundalis, pp. 129-131. (2006)
All images reprinted with permission.

Cataloguing-in-Publication Data

Blass, Fred R., 1960 –
Levy, David A., 1964 –
Parco, James E. 1968 –
       The 52nd floor: thinking deeply about leadership / 1st ed.
       232 p., 23 cm.
       Includes bibliographical references and index
       IBSN: 978-0-9820185-3-8 (paperback)
       1. Leadership   2. Organization   3. Executive ability   4. Creative ability
       in business   I. Title: 52nd floor.   II. Title

HD57.7.F444 2008   LCCN: 2008937968
658.4'092-dc22

TABLE OF CONTENTS

A Journey Into Culture

A Journey Into Control

A Journey Into Understanding

PREFACE

W e believe that this book is unique and has the potential to be transformative. Together, we've devoted our working lives to helping students and clients understand the nature of organizations at multiple levels. Over the years we've learned that the traditional techniques such as lectures, PowerPoint™ presentations, and having our students and clients memorize lists does not work because all is soon forgotten. The world doesn't need another set of "indisputable" laws or principles. It is our understanding that the only indisputable law is the fact that organizations and the people in them undergo constant change. What works today may not tomorrow and the only people that have a chance to figure out what will work are those who possess the knowledge, skills and attitudes necessary to embrace and facilitate change. Great leaders are those who have a refined ability to adapt to change. The greater your adaptive capacity, the more likely you are to develop creative solutions to complex and ambiguous organizational problems. Increasing your adaptive capacity is what we aim to do with this book.

We offer you the most effective approach to learning about leadership we've found that works. We offer you stories and inquiry. Think about your school years or seminars you've recently attended. *What do you remember?* If you're like our students, you remember the stories that were told to you and how you thought about them afterwards. The stories stick because they resonate and can bring us to new frames of reference and insight. In short, stories coupled with reflection provide a gateway to deeper understanding.

Stories are nothing new. Great stories can inspire us and provide the cornerstones for a journey of reflection and inquiry. Without a reflective aspect, they may only amuse, but with guided reflection, stories can become transformative. Just as many religious traditions use the method of reading a short passage from a sacred text followed by guided questions for reflection, we bring this tradition into the study of leadership and organizational life. What is often lacking in the day-to-day operations of organizations – corporate, nonprofit, or government – is a habit of practiced reflection.

Thinking deeply takes time and effort. The fact is that people are very busy, so busy they usually have little to no time to reflect upon their thinking. Using the stories in this book, we hope to engage you in a topic. Then, with a series of questions that follow each story, guide you on a journey into your own thinking to enhance your understanding of leadership.

Leadership is about influencing others. By learning how to recognize interdependencies as a source of power within organizational settings, we can refine our skills to influence others more adeptly. But don't think of this as a one-way street. Just as a boss influences his or her employees, employees can also influence their boss. Leadership cannot be discovered, acquired and possessed; rather, it just *is*. In fact, we don't believe leadership is a concept that can be readily defined and understood. No irrefutable laws or principles exist except those that you discover to be true for you. To the extent you improve your knowledge, skills and attitudes about what leadership is, the more likely you will influence those around you. Just as leadership is not a linear concept and cannot effectively be approached as such, the same holds true for this book.

There are many ways you can engage this book. The first and most obvious would be to start at the beginning, read each story and rifle through the questions. While this will certainly make for a quick read, it will likely be of little value. Remember, this is a book that uses reflection as a method to help you discover how you *think about your thinking* as it pertains to organizational leadership. Reflection takes time. Thus, we suggest that you spend most of your time with the questions. Read them, allow your mind to go wherever the questions take you, and then try to figure out why you came up with the thoughts you did. Also, try to be aware of your emotional reactions to the questions and ask yourself why you might feel the way you do as you ponder a particular question or story. Are you reacting to the question or is the question uncovering something within you that you do not want to see or acknowledge? We believe if you approach the questions in this way, you will find them somewhat challenging. *Yes-no* or *right-wrong* answers are rare. Once you think you've answered a question completely, consider whether the opposite of your answer might also be true from a different perspective. Some of the questions can't be answered, and yet they still demand an answer. We know. We've been working with them for years. In writing this book, we have spent more time trying to *ask the right questions* than with any other part of the text. We believe that a similar effort will be required on your part in answering them if you truly want to expand your understanding of organizational realities.

We encourage you to write in the book and make any notes you feel that are warranted. After all, one important objective of this book is to help you to understand your own thinking. Yes, of course, we were often taught not to write in our textbooks. That was because the teacher didn't want us to highlight the answers for the next reader. Not to worry here. It's okay because there are no correct answers other than what *you believe* to be correct from your own analysis. Memorizing principles, laws and lists often creates an illusion of knowledge. If only leadership were that simple, but it's not. You are in the best position to determine what will work for you and for your organization. As we journey through this book, we hope to *ask you the right questions* in a manner that guides you into thinking deeply about leadership.

D.L. J.P. F.B.

———❦———

INTRODUCTION

*D*oes leadership exist?

Is that the right question? What do we really want to know when we ask a question like this? People rarely think deeply about the questions they ask. How a question is asked necessarily frames the boundaries of possible answers. And once a quest begins to find a right answer, the question often goes unquestioned from that point forward.

Consider how many times you received answers that you didn't like. How did you react? Did you find yourself becoming disgusted with the person answering the question? Or did you find yourself becoming disgusted with the question? We believe asking the correct question is vital because the structure of the question often dictates the quality of answer. *Ask the right question* and you may discover the correct answer. Ask wrong questions and you'll get wrong answers every time.

What is leadership? This is a great example of a wrong question. Does it matter how we answer it? Let's see. Suppose we define leadership as "character, competence and charisma." By our definition, to demonstrate leadership, you must exhibit these three characteristics. But what about "compassion?" Should leaders be *"compassionate"*? Again, another wrong question. Suppose we add "compassion" to our definition. Is the definition better? Perhaps. But what about *"cowardice"*? Leaders should be *"courageous,"right?* So let's add "courage." You can see where this is going – nowhere. Yet, this is precisely what is often done today in book after book on leadership.

Does leadership exist? Consider the question. Is this a better question? If we could come up with a universally agreed-upon definition describing what leadership is and isn't, then we could make the case that leadership *does* exist. But if we can't, we might be asking a wrong question. A better question might be, *"Why do we have such a difficult time defining leadership?"* Maybe because it is not a concept that lends itself to definition, but rather a guiding set of ideas that helps us exert influence over others in pursuit of a common objective.

We believe a journey into leadership depends upon inquiry and enactment rather than definitions and principles. That's right, you have to create it. You can't read a book to understand leadership. You have to write your own. As a first step on this journey, we must begin to understand the complexity of relationships that exist in organizational settings. Ultimately, we need to develop an astute understanding of how people in our organizations act and react to a variety of stimuli. Sometimes the stimulus is an external force; other times, it might not be obvious where the stimulus is coming from.

The organizational reality isn't necessarily one that exists requiring navigation on our part. The interconnectedness among people in an organization implies that if one person is affected, so is everyone else. What most people tend to overlook is that *they* are part of the system. They are a stimulus. They are a force. Instead, we are *co-creators* of that reality. Once we recognize the power we have to influence others, so many things that never made sense before come into view with precision and clarity. The stories that you are about to read attempt to demonstrate this.

Recognizing our roles as creative actors in a system isn't necessarily sufficient to have the level of influence we might desire. Understanding how best to influence the people in your organization, be it your boss, your assistant, or the guy in the cubicle across the hall, requires knowing what the sources of power are and how to discover them. Like leadership, power is more than a definition. Power is a function of dependencies. We believe there are strong connections between leadership, power, culture and control. By reflecting on the stories, we hope that you will discover how to embrace these connections for yourself, and create a leadership approach that works best for you in the unique context of your organization.

———⊸≫≪⊶———

DISCLAIMER

This book is designed to take you on a journey into a deeper understanding of leadership. From undergraduates to senior executives, *students of leadership* are similar in that they are typically very bright, exceptionally motivated and ultimately committed to being the very best they can be. Such people are not easily fooled and normally believe that useful knowledge is that which can be applied to make them better leaders. We believe that they are correct. We have learned through our own journeys as professional educators that the best academic courses are never those where professors peddle answers to their students. Students tend to judge leadership courses far more favorably when professors ask very specific questions that help them discover meaning for themselves. Such an approach, however, can create an ambiguous, and sometimes frustrating context where many things are possible rather than a single *correct* answer dictated by the teacher. Thus, we have structured this book to recreate such an experience here. Some degree of frustration is both inevitable and essential if a level of deep thinking is to be achieved. This is our goal.

Thus, unlike many other leadership books, you will not find any models, lists or infallible principles here. Although you will be introduced to many critical concepts, the real value will not be obtained by committing these concepts to memory, but instead by developing a deep understanding of the *interrelationships* between them. We are confident that readers will develop the same level of excitement and appreciation of the material after they have taken it in and digested it as we have.

Within each section of the book, you will encounter a group of stories. At the end of each story, you will find questions. For most of these questions, there really are no *right* or *wrong* answers. Due to their reflective nature, these questions are intended to prime your thinking about the issues raised and then help you to *think deeply – to think critically*. The questions are designed to get you to reflect on what you already know, thereby *expanding* what you know. *Reflection* is the key to gaining value from this book.

If you find yourself turning a page and not finding an answer that you believe should be there, we ask that you be patient and continue on the journey. We anticipate that in time you will discover far more than you might otherwise expect.

Following each group of stories in a section, you will find what we consider to be a higher-level question that relates to the group of stories as a whole with a brief discussion highlighting some of the more salient aspects. Then, in the *Authors' Reflections* section, we collectively share with you our thoughts, opinions and expertise on each of the stories. Again, we want to emphasize that you probably will not find answers to all of the questions, but rather our perspectives regarding what differentiates leaders – good from great, effective from ineffective.

For those of you who might desire an extended academic discussion on a particular topic beyond the scope of this book, we have also included an appendix of some of the more profound works directly relating to the topics presented (see *Appendix A* – which also includes a suggested reading list at the end.)

Above all else, just as we tell our students and clients, our purpose is to create value by helping others to do the same for themselves. In writing this book, we have done our very best to help readers think more deeply about an immensely important topic.

Only you can be the judge of how well we have done.

A JOURNEY INTO LEADERSHIP

"Leadership is the art of getting someone else to do something you want done because he wants to do it."
—Dwight Eisenhower

"If your actions inspire others to dream more, learn more, do more and become more, you are a leader."
—John Quincy Adams

"Leadership and learning are indispensable to each other."
—John F. Kennedy

"The first responsibility of a leader is to define reality."
—Max DePree

LEADERSHIP BY THE BOOK

The Executive MBA program had a rare treat in store for the students that weekend. A famous Gulf War general was going to speak to them about *leadership*. After the young professor introduced him, the general, with shiny stars and colorful medals, addressed the crowd. *"The first thing I want to tell you – and it is important – is that you can't learn leadership from a book."* The whole class turned and stared at the professor. The professor knew what was going through their minds, *"If you can't learn leadership from a book, what the hell are we doing here?"* Instead of responding, the professor just shrugged.

The general continued,

> *"You can learn 'about leadership' from books. Learning 'about leadership' and 'leading' are two very different concepts. It's one thing to learn about swimming. You can learn about different types of strokes, about which goggles offer the least water resistance, about proper cadence and breathing, but those are all very different from the act of swimming. Just as it may be helpful for a swimmer to read a book about swimming, reading about leadership may be helpful to those engaged in leading. Please don't expect to become a great leader by sitting in this class. No offense to your teacher. If you want to be a great leader, practice the art of leading. You practice, you observe, you reflect, you adapt and you start the cycle over and over again. It is an intensely private affair. I say it is private because it all boils down to your inner experience of the context you are operating in. It's private in that sense, but public in the sense that it is engaged with others out in the open for everyone to see and scrutinize.*

Oh yeah, one other thing I should mention. The act of leading is a process that undergoes constant change. When you find what works, such as your "six keys to success," you'll eventually fail. All the elements in a leadership situation are constantly changing. You as a leader are growing and changing. Your workforce is developing. Some employees leave the organization, others enter it. The situation changes all the time. The easiest way for a leader to fail is for him or her to apply what worked yesterday to today.

I want you to understand that I did not learn this from a book. You can read it in a book, but you need to experience it for yourself for it to do you any good. Good luck to you as you become our future leaders."

Reflections:

° What can you learn about leadership from a book?

° What is the role of reflection in becoming a more competent leader?

° Can learning take place without reflection?

(Authors' Reflections on page 32)

THE ELDERLY GENTLEMAN

Since the elderly gentleman with a head of white and unruly hair was once a very powerful CEO of a Fortune 100 company, he was invited to give a talk on leadership to a group of senior executives. He started by describing the powerful vision he developed for his former company and how it drove change over the years. He talked about hiring good people that could be trusted, empowerment, and started describing the tough decisions that leaders must make on a regular basis. Then there was a long pause and the old man looked confused. He started speaking again, then stopped. After several uncomfortable moments and with a sad look on his face he said, *"I'm sorry. I don't think I can continue this speech. The truth is that I don't think leadership exists."*

The senior executives looked at one another and knew what each other was thinking. Here was a truly great man – a giant among giants – an exceptional leader who was now in decline. His once sharp mind was faltering and it was painful to watch. In the back of everyone's mind was the same question, *"Will this happen to me one day, too?"* The elderly man continued:

> *"Believers in leadership can recite many phrases, slogans and variants of definitions regarding what they think leadership is, but it is always used to describe what happened in the past. Actually, it's a bit of a tautology. Companies that have done well are said to have had great leadership. Poorly performing companies have had poor leadership. None can reliably tell us where it is going to be, how it will get there, and most importantly, whether it will succeed once it arrives. I'm not saying that leaders don't exist; I'm not that crazy, yet. Leadership? Damned if I have a clue?"*

The expression on the faces of the senior executives seemed to shift from sadness to confusion.

Reflections:

- ° Can you define leadership? If so, would everybody agree with your definition?

- ° Imagine if the word "leadership" was removed from the English language, what knowledge would be lost?

(Authors' Reflections on page 33)

THE MANIFESTO

As John followed Pat into the office, Pat slammed the door in frustration and said, *"I can't believe the way Mitch humiliated Tony during the staff meeting. He even seemed to enjoy it and laid it on thicker when Tony got flustered."* John nodded in agreement as he recalled the way Mitch seemed to take perverse pleasure in verbally abusing Tony.

After a moment of silent reflection Pat continued, *"You know, this makes me sick. For some reason incomprehensible to me, it is perfectly legal to be a horrible leader. Leaders cannot be arrested for ignoring their employees or for being completely indifferent to their needs. Leaders don't have to care about people. Leaders have no legal responsibility to develop or nurture their employees. Leaders do not have to treat employees as human beings. People have come to be viewed as resources – human resources. They are to be managed and used like other company resources, to be maintained and consumed by the organization. When the human resource no longer adds value to the company's bottom line, it is to be salvaged with the outdated computers, old office furniture, and the dried up correction fluid. The way Mitch treated Tony ought to be illegal."*

John walked over to his whiteboard, grabbed a marker and said, *"So, what would a 'Good Leader Law' look like?"*

"Huh?" replied Pat a bit taken aback. *"Oh, I wasn't serious. After all, laws can't prohibit bad leaders from being in charge."*

"Maybe not," said John. *"But let's just pretend for a moment that there was such a law. What would it look like?"*

Pat paused for a moment and then started by saying, *"Well, I think that leaders must treat their employees as people as well as resources. I'm not a computer. I'm a living human being and should be treated accordingly."*

John replied, *"Yeah, that's a good point. But leaders should also trust their employees unless given a specific reason not to such as lying, cheating or stealing from the company."*

Pat nodded. *"True. I agree and I also think that leaders must demonstrate through their actions that they care about the well-being of their employees, because I remember last year when I came to work sick as a dog and Mitch just kept squeezing sanitizer on his hands rather than tell me to go home and get some rest. How can the guy lead us without giving a damn about us? It's pathetic that we want to try to force him to be a decent human being. It's even more pathetic that he likely will never do the right thing unless he's forced to do so."*

John smiled. *"Good point, but you know the thing that bothers me most is when they look down their nose at the people they lead as though we are less intelligent or somehow less entitled than they are. They must treat those that follow them with equal respect and dignity."*

The conversation continued and after forty-five minutes of wishful thinking they came up with their Good Leader Law:

1. Leaders must treat their followers as people as well as resources.

2. Leaders must trust their people unless given a specific reason not to.

3. Leaders must demonstrate through their actions that they care about the well-being of their people.

4. Leaders must treat those that follow them with respect and dignity.

5. Leaders must listen to their stakeholders and acknowledge that they've listened.

6. Leaders must make a genuine effort to know as many people's names in the organization as possible.

7. Leaders must demonstrate through their responsible actions that they are competent stewards of social systems that are bigger than they are.

8. Leaders must be adaptive and acknowledge that they are willing to continuously learn.

9. Leaders, as stewards of their organizational system, must continuously work to improve that system for the benefit of all people in the system as well as the system itself.

10. Leaders must continuously reflect on how to become a better leader.

Perhaps the leaders of today have it easy.

Reflections:

- ° Would you vote for a Good Leader Law?

- ° What should be added? Removed?

- ° What does a leader need to do to create an environment where such a law would be entirely unnecessary?

(Authors' Reflections on page 34)

SELFISH BEHAVIOR

Two CEOs were talking to each other about their employees. The first CEO complained about how selfish his employees were. He talked about the tremendous positive impact his medical supply company was having on the lives of millions of people. He was frustrated that most of his employees didn't seem to care about this and were only interested in their individual lives and careers. Out of desperation he asked the other CEO, *"What can I do to get my people to be less selfish?"*

The other CEO, without hesitation, said, *"Why don't YOU be selfish for them? If your employees know that you are defending and fighting for their interests, then they will realize that their interests are aligned with those of the organization. Think about it."*

Reflections:

- ° What is the second CEO really trying to say?

- ° Why do we typically view selfishness as a negative behavior?

- ° To what extent is someone being selfish when they enjoy what they do?

- ° What can a leader do to assure his followers that he has their selfish interests in mind?

- ° How can a leader align selfish interests with organizational interests?

(Authors' Reflections on page 35)

DEAR JOHN

John had been with the organization for over ten years. He had won every award, received the highest evaluations, and only wanted to stay with the company and continue doing what he did so well. He turned down opportunities for promotion because he loved his job and he was better at it than anyone else. His boss, the division manager, said he was exceptionally talented and would do anything for him. In fact, she believed that he should transfer to another division as it would potentially set him up to be her successor. He was appreciative and flattered but was honest with her and stated plainly that he had no ambition to entertain such a move. He felt certain he would be quite content for many years to come in his present job. As far as he could tell, it was probably the best situation for him as well as the organization.

Six months after the discussion with his boss, he received the paperwork transferring him to the other division. The news was completely unexpected and he was disappointed. He had little interest in the new job, and he honestly did not feel that he had the technical competence needed. But he was a good company man and said little to his peers or superiors about his true feelings. In fact, when asked (or rather, consoled) about the transfer by his work mates, he punctuated it merely as "a great opportunity" and soon everyone in the division was happy for John.

John had a very close friend, Mark, with whom he had worked side-by-side for the past four years. Mark was a very insightful and quiet person. Mark summed the entire issue up in a two-sentence e-mail sent to John on the day he left the division. It read:

"Dear John, I am a spiritual person, and I believe everything happens for a reason. In your case, it's poor leadership."

Reflections:

- ° Who knew what was better for John? John or his boss?

- ° Who knew what was better for the organization? John or his boss?

- ° When opinions of advancement collide, who should determine the outcome?

- ° Why does advancement always seem to be the desired end-state?

- ° To what extent do we create our own organizational realities?

(Authors' Reflections on page 36)

THE THESPIAN

The senior executive was loved by all seven of his immediate staff. Each one over the years had built a strong relationship of mutual trust with him. Beyond that, they felt blessed to have a boss that truly understood and liked them. They knew it was rare to find a person that could understand others as this boss did. They could go to him with any problem, personal problems included, and he'd show compassion and empathy. Even better was that his advice usually helped. It wasn't just a show. He really cared.

One day, two of the employees were sitting in an office chatting about their boss when one of them became confused. Bob said, *"Wait a second, what did the boss tell you?"* Susan responded, *"It's like I just said – he was telling me how critically important it is for the company to have those end of the month status reports."*

"Are you kidding me?" said Bob. *"Two days ago he was agreeing with me when I was complaining that those status reports are a waste of time. All the data is available in real-time on the intranet. Why would he tell you that they're important? He knows they're a waste of time."*

Susan was now getting angry. *"They're not a waste of time. It would take the boss twenty minutes to find the information on the intranet. It's so much better to have all the information compiled into one document every month for him. You know how he is all about efficiency and it's more efficient for our division to compile the report."*

Bob looked puzzled. *"That's not the boss I know. He hates all the time wasted on reports that serve no other purpose than making a few people look good. You don't know him at all."*

All the commotion drew the attention of Ken who had been listening to the discussion nearby. He interjected, *"Obviously, neither of you know our boss. If you did, you'd realize that he believes in be-*

ing the boss that each of us needs. If the status report is important to you, it is important to him. If it's not important to you, it's not important to him."

"So you're saying the boss is two-faced?", asked Susan.

Ken smiled, *"Aren't we all?"*

Reflections:

- ° Do you act the same way around everyone you know?

- ° Do you treat your mother the same as you treat your boss? Why not?

- ° Is there a real you or is "you" defined by your relationships with others?

- ° What does it mean to be the boss that each person needs?

- ° How can you be the leader everyone wants while also being the leader that everyone needs?

(Authors' Reflections on page 37)

WHAT IS LEADERSHIP?

This is the wrong question. No matter how authors might attempt to define leadership, the simple truth is that most books on leadership leave us in the same place we started. Because the concept of "leadership" can be defined in terms of almost any positive attribute, character trait, or behavior, it becomes useless as a prescriptive guide to help an aspiring young leader develop his or her leadership potential by trying to discover what leadership *is*. No matter how hard we look, how much we read, or how many seminars we attend on leadership, in the end all we are usually left with is someone's latest "model," a story of someone's unique personal experience or a list of good things to practice and bad things to avoid. *But is that leadership?*

An Amazon.com search reveals over 267,000 books on leadership. Why are there so many books on this topic? Shouldn't someone have written *the* book on leadership by now making all the other books obsolete, or at least redundant? Don't they all say almost the same thing? Why do people read books on leadership? We used to believe people read books on leadership to learn *about* leadership. We now realize it was an incorrect assumption.

A few years ago we had the opportunity to attend a seminar led by a best-selling author of a book on leadership. As it turned out, we were somewhat disappointed by the seminar as it was not much different from the book. Yet, to our surprise, the majority of the attendees seemed to be enamored with it. They leaned forward as the author spoke and continuously nodded their heads in agreement. The discussion afterwards consisted mostly of superficial questions and answers. When it was all over, there was elation and a standing ovation. This came as quite a surprise to us because we could not discern the value which so many others seemed to grasp.

We spent the next few months trying to make sense of what had happened. We eventually came to the conclusion that most of us do not read books and attend seminars on leadership to learn about leadership. It is more likely we engage leadership books and leadership seminars for the validation and comfort value they provide. Organizations are incredibly complex, immensely intricate systems that largely defy understanding. We can't accurately predict the behavior of a single person, let alone the activities of hundreds or thousands of people working together within an organization. Coupled with competing stakeholder interests, an ever-changing organizational environment and an uncertain future and one can easily go crazy with the daunting task of *leadership*. After all, leaders are stewards of their organizational systems and are responsible for its efficient performance, growth and maintenance. A checklist of absolutes regarding leadership would be a dream come true for any leader as it would bring clarity to the role of leadership. Every leader would be able to say, *"I'm a great leader because I have a vision and book X says great leaders have a vision."*

If you are looking for comfort or validation commonly found in other leadership books, it is likely you will be disappointed here. We don't believe the concept of *leadership* is as simple as it is often made to appear. Instead, we believe a true understanding of leadership emerges from a firm awareness of how unique you and your organization are from any other context. Not only do each of us find ourselves in unique situations as leaders, to make matters worse, everything is constantly changing. Because *you* will change, *your* organization will change, and *your* environment will change, to be a highly effective leader, you must constantly think deeply about the connections between you, your organization and all of people in which you interact. Because *leadership is really about you,* you'll have to do most of the work for yourself through reflection and inquiry.

AUTHOR REFLECTIONS... *On Leadership*

Leadership by the Book (p.18)

We believe leadership is about engagement. Engagement involves inquiry, reflection and interaction with an organizational system. It's true that reading about swimming is far different from the act of swimming and it would be hard to read about swimming while fluttering around in a pool of water. Leaders do have the luxury, however, of reading books on leadership while at the helm of an organizational system. So, if leaders are careful, they can read about leadership while leading and not drown in the process. There is still a problem, though. No book on leadership can ever capture the complexities of organizational life. Organizations are dynamic systems. Thus, any descriptive analysis would immediately become historical analysis because the system would have already changed once observed. Leaders must not only continually adapt to the systems they've created, they must also continuously adapt the organizational systems to the leaders' continuous adaptation. Books can help us better understand the complex relationships which leaders face, but the essence of what it takes to effectively lead must be discovered and rediscovered by each of us for ourselves.

We also believe reflecting on leadership is critical for leaders. To the extent a book can help with reflection, then it is likely useful. Biographies, which are nothing more than a collection of connected stories, are particularly helpful. What should be obvious by now is how partial we are to stories because of the meaning they can communicate to the astute reader. If nothing else, it gives the student of leadership the appreciation that leadership is *context dependent*. Mahatma Gandhi, George S. Patton and Jack Welch were all "great leaders" in their own right, but imagine Patton in India, Gandhi trying to run GE and Welch trying to lead the 3rd Army during WWII in Germany. We also think it is useful for students to *read about* the various "leadership theories." Be it a trait-based, behavioral-based or transformational theory, each model can be useful in identifying relationships between leaders, followers, goals, and environments. These relationships are often critical to a leader's perspective when working to influence others. One can surely become a great leader without reading leadership books, especially if he or she has competent mentors and opportunities to *practice leading*. For those less fortunate, reading is a way to exercise deliberate reflection and engage in the essential inquiry.

Elderly Gentleman (p.20)

Supreme Court Justice Potter Stewart once commented in a landmark case dealing with pornography, *"It's hard to define, but I know it when I see it."* Although the same thing can probably be said about leadership, such a pronouncement is of little help to organizations that are deeply committed to teaching leadership and developing leaders.

For decades, organizations spent millions of dollars trying to determine what leadership is. In fact, during the 1980s and 1990s, major firms reported "leadership consulting" as one of their single largest efforts, yet what more do we know now about what leadership is as compared to before?

Many organizations eventually came to realize it was time wasted and money poorly spent to continue pursuing the Holy Grail of an all encompassing theory of leadership. Instead, the focus shifted to *what leaders do* and *how to create them*. What organizations really need are processes to attract the most talented individuals, develop them to their maximum potential and then create systems to retain them. The task is fundamental, but the art of perfecting it is forever elusive as the complexity and ambiguity of organizational environments is ever-changing. All of us have the capacity to be a leader, but only those among us who can develop their potential to effectively influence others are worthy of the title.

The relationship between leaders and leadership is similar to the relationship between being human and "humanship." Not surprisingly, the word "humanship" doesn't exist. If it did we would expect it to mean the practice or function of being human. The word adds no meaning since everything a human being does is the function or act of being human. With *leadership*, we have the same relationship. Everything a legitimate leader does in the organization falls under being a leader. There are no boundaries separating the human being as a leader and the human being as a non-leader. The policies the leader makes, her articulation of those policies, her appearance and how she relates to her appearance, her interactions, smiles, frowns, energy or lack of energy all impact the organization at both conscious and unconscious levels and cannot be separated from the leader. The complexity of interactions between the leader and organization, which has a reciprocal effect on the leader, is beyond human comprehension. This is largely why we find books which "lay out the laws of leadership" to be trivial at best and harmful at their worst. It's also probably why we don't find any books on "humanship."

Our judgment of the quality of leadership is usually an attribution based on our innate need to follow. We want to know someone is in charge. We want to make our own attributions of success and failure based on their actions. We want to feel as though our fate is left to purposeful action more than mere happenstance.

Someone may be a good leader, yet we might assign them accountability for all of the "bad" we perceive, or they may be a poor leader to which we attribute all the good we perceive. The point is, to the extent we feel someone influences outcomes, then we label them as leaders.

The Manifesto (p.22)

It is doubtful a Good Leader Law would have much impact. Most leaders go to work each day genuinely wanting to do good things for their organizations and those who work for them. They see themselves as "very good leaders," yet if you ask their followers, you may find a difference of opinion. Whether someone is a "good" or "bad" leader is often a matter of perspective and we are left to wonder, by whose perspective should we judge merit?

Instead of a Good Leader Law, perhaps instead we could instead ask leaders to take an oath. Consider something like this:

> *"As this organization's leader, I am first and foremost a human being. I have feelings, goals and motivations to do good things for my organization and society. I will make mistakes, and when I do, I will immediately work to fix them as soon as I become aware of them. I will remain accountable for my actions. I will not use my position as a leader to influence individuals in my organization to make other people feel like they are not as good or worthy as me because I believe everyone who works for me is trustworthy and honorable. Their standards are as high as mine. Their integrity is beyond reproach. I trust them completely and without reservation. They can trust me in exactly the same way."*

Imagine a world where leaders would attest to the truth of this oath publicly before their organization and then remain accountable to it for the duration of their tenure as the leader. From a systems perspective, more rules, laws or oaths might be the last thing most organizations need. One thing is certain: organizations need leaders who are committed to inclusion and respect of all who work for them.

Selfish Behavior (p.25)

Thomas Hobbes probably got it more right than wrong in 1651 with his book *Leviathan* illustrating how human behavior is inherently self-interested.[1] We're all selfish and generally behave in our own best interests. Sometimes it is in our best interest to engage in selfless behavior. We might feel good about engaging in activities from which we derive no tangible benefit. We love to do meaningful work, work which serves our communities, societies, or mankind. We are more free to do this meaningful work in an organization when we know our boss is looking out for us and will give us the promotions, bonuses, and challenging projects we deserve. When the boss takes care of our organizational needs, we can engage in those selfless activities which make us feel so good.

In the *Selfish Behavior* story, perhaps both CEOs were correct. The first was correct in observing how all of his employees are selfish. At least he is aware of what is going on in his organization. The second CEO is also correct. She has a far more sophisticated understanding of selfishness. She takes selfishness as given, and then tries to put mechanisms in place to leverage the selfishness and align it with organizational goals. To the extent leaders care for their people's needs, the more likely he or she will be an effective leader.

Leadership involves knowing yourself, knowing others, and knowing the situation. Because reading and reflection can help us achieve a deeper understanding of organizational complexity, it is a worthwhile endeavor. Perhaps the greatest challenge from this perspective is thinking deeply enough to truly know ourselves. We are constantly adapting to others and to our environments. Our attitudes change, our perception of others changes, and even our perspective of leadership changes. Leaders also develop through stages from infancy to maturity. Reading about "stages of leadership" in a book can provide great insights and opportunity for reflection, but cannot be a substitute for the visceral experience.

Dear John (p.26)

During the last century, traditional hierarchical organizations were often led by dictatorial bosses who made all the decisions. The best boss one could hope for in those days was a paternalistic dictator who pretended to care for his employees. He would make career decisions for his employees and they would have to assume the decisions were correct. Sometimes they were and sometimes they weren't, but during an era where a life-long commitment to a particular employer was the norm, it didn't matter. Employees had been socialized to serve a particular company for the duration of their work life. Those days are long gone, but not everyone got the word. New generations of workers are redefining the very boundaries of what constitutes work life. While good employees have good options, great employees have great options. If leaders wish to effectively attract and maintain talent, they will need to understand their employees' needs better than ever before.

The Thespian (p.28)

When we use this story with students and clients they immediately gravitate to how disingenuous the leader is and how he will likely lose the respect of his subordinates. When we reveal that we know the person in which *The Thespian* story is based on and agree he's one of the best leaders we've ever encountered, the reply is usually something like *"If he is so good, how can he get away with acting like this?"* It's a fair question, but to fully appreciate the sophistication of *The Thespian*, we must pay attention to the different levels in which he is communicating.

The leader in this story certainly treats everyone differently at the individual level. As the story suggests, he tries to be the leader each employee *wants* because each employee has different *needs*. If you step up to a higher level, however, you see a leader completely committed to the mission of the organization – a leader who values all employees equally – a leader who knows his employees well enough to be able to treat them differently. Since they know this about the leader, employees trust him without reservation and assume his actions are in the best interests of both the organization and the individuals. This is certainly easier said than done, but if you can pull it off, you could be viewed as a hero.

A JOURNEY INTO POWER

"Nearly all men can stand adversity, but if you want to test a man's character, give him power."
—Abraham Lincoln

"Being powerful is like being a lady. If you have to tell people you are, you aren't."
—Margaret Thatcher

"Perhaps those who are best suited to power are those who have never sought it."
—Albus Dumbledore

THE GURU

Sixty-five people flew from all over the world to attend the Guru's week-long spiritual development seminar. The morning started at sunrise with an hour of meditation. Following that was a wonderful vegetarian breakfast with strong black coffee and tea. The morning sessions were led by the Guru's assistants, many of whom were highly-qualified teachers themselves. Next, came a lovely vegetarian lunch followed by an hour or two of personal time. The Guru arrived at mid-afternoon and stayed with the group until early evening. He had been trained over many decades in an Eastern tradition of spirituality but now saw his purpose as bringing this wisdom to the West without unnecessary baggage. Sitting on a hardwood floor might be perceived to be unnecessary baggage. So, not surprisingly, everyone was seated in chairs.

The time with the Guru was special for everyone present. He started each session with a question-and-answer period. Questions often involved extremely personal issues that people had been dealing with for years. Next came a series of experiential exercises followed by a discussion led by the Guru. After two and a half hours, the Guru thanked everyone for coming and left the spiritual center. The group was on its own to find dinner and had the option of attending an evening meditation session.

On the fourth day of the seminar, everyone was abuzz with what happened with the Guru on the previous day. During the question-and-answer period, a woman had asked the Guru a question and then immediately broke down and wept. After a moment, she became very angry and began weeping again. Everyone in the crowd was caught up in her emotional state and was wondering how the Guru was going to deal with this unexpected problem. Using his incredible intuition, the Guru immediately started asking her questions to calm her down. Even though he was working very intimately and deeply with her, it was clear to everyone that her problem was far from resolved. Realizing this, the Guru gave the woman an exercise to work on and said he'd readdress her problem at the end of the day's session. The Guru moved on and started working with the larger group. He left that evening without speaking to the woman again.

During the first session the following morning, the first question, the only question on everyone's mind was, *"What happened with the woman from the previous day?"* Several people started pointing out the skillful means of the Guru, stating it was brilliant to let her work out her problem on her own without relying on the Guru as a crutch. Everyone agreed. One assistant noted that no one can solve another's problems. In the end, we have to live our own lives. He suggested that someone ask the Guru why he chose not to address her again when he came to visit the session that afternoon.

As expected, the first question asked of the Guru when the afternoon session began was *"Can you explain the skillful means you used by never coming back to the emotional woman yesterday?"*

The Guru responded, *"Oh crap! I forgot about her."*

Reflections:

   ° Do you know leaders who can do no wrong?

   ° What is it that creates the perception of others' infallibility regardless of what they say?

   ° How are you perceived by other people? How do you know?

   ° How much control do you have over what people think?

   ° What specific things can you do to manage what other people think of you?

(Authors' Reflections on page 57)

LAYING DOWN THE LAW

Gary was used to wielding power. At 6'4" and a former linebacker for his college football team, he was an imposing figure. He'd been that way since elementary school when he first started throwing his size around. Now, although he still liked to make his presence known when he walked into a room by puffing-up his chest and holding his arms out to the side a bit (as if his massive muscles were preventing him from a natural body posture), he'd found other means to show his strength.

As a new vice president, Gary took charge. He spent several weeks reviewing all of the previous VP's policies and procedures. Then he set down the law by rewriting them all. Most of the changes really didn't change anything. They were tweaks to previous procedures that would be noticed if they weren't followed, but didn't really change outcomes. Gary used them as a test of his leadership, of his ability to get his people to follow him. As he became more and more familiar with his new organization, he started to write policies that were a significant departure from previous procedures. Some would argue that these policies were moving in the wrong direction, that they made their work unnecessarily complicated and restrictive. Most would argue that they didn't add any value and were just a nuisance.

To Gary, his policies and procedures were incredibly important. They were *his* policies and procedures. They were a manifestation of his power. His philosophy has always been *"use it or lose it"* when it came to power. He'd seen too many vice presidents act indecisively or go with the flow only to find their employees taking advantage of them. Vice presidents, he felt, were meant to exert power and leadership. Making rules and setting standards are what good leaders do. At least that's what he thought until he met Chuck.

Chuck was a bad seed. He was a lower-level employee but was also an informal leader among his peers. His attitude was terrible and he did his best to poison everyone around him. He'd bad mouth the company and the boss constantly, turn peers against each other and instigate trouble whenever he thought he could get away with it. It would be hard to estimate the amount of damage Chuck did to the company, but it was certainly substantial.

Gary saw Chuck as a weed in an otherwise immaculate garden. He wanted to pluck the weed as soon as possible. The problem was that Chuck was untouchable. Gary made rules for just about every-thing and Chuck always made sure that he followed the rules. His work was never great, sometimes good, but always above the mini-mum standard set forth in Gary's rules. Chuck could be malicious, but he was obedient.

Reflections:

° Who has more power, Gary or Chuck? Why?

° Who are the most powerful people in your organiza-tion?

° Do they tend to use their power more for the organiza-tion or for themselves?

° How much power do you have in your organization?

° Do you tend to use it more for the organization or for yourself?

° How might you lose power by using it?

(Authors' Reflections on page 57)

THE COFFEE MAKER

Power can assume so many forms. With over twenty-five years of experience in the military, thousands of hours as a command pilot and a commander of four combat units, Colonel Johnson was a man accustomed to power. As a final assignment before retirement, Col. Johnson was selected to command a Reserve Officers' Training Corps (ROTC) detachment at a major college campus. His primary responsibility would be to guide the training of several dozen cadets to become future officers. It seemed like this should have been the easiest job for a man of his stature. But it wasn't. This job was way outside of the colonel's comfort zone. There would be no large military base at his disposal, no large staff, and no flying. Three junior captains, a sergeant and a secretary comprised the entire realm of his leadership domain.

Upon his arrival on campus, Colonel Johnson quickly realized that he knew less about the training program than anyone in the office, including the secretary. Being a wise man, he realized that he should let his people do their jobs since they knew what they were doing better than he did. So, he sat in his office. The truth be told, it was a smart thing to do since the detachment had recently been told that it was the top-rated unit in the country. That's #1 out of 143 units. The only place to go from there was down. This drove Colonel Johnson crazy. It must have driven him crazy because if he wasn't crazy, the incident wouldn't have happened. You could see it in his eyes, *"But this isn't what leaders do. Leadership is about taking action!"*

Everything started off as a normal weekly staff meeting. Each of the captains briefed the colonel on his or her area of responsibility. As usual, the colonel nodded his head, made a few comments, but did not direct any changes. At the end of the meeting the sergeant happened to comment that they needed a new coffee machine and asked the colonel if he could buy one and get reimbursed. All hell broke loose. The colonel wanted to know model numbers, costs, features and the quality of various coffee-maker brands. One of the captains went back to his office and grabbed fliers from last Sunday's paper.

Before anyone knew what had happened, fliers were scattered across the conference room table and Sears and JC Penny catalogs were being explored. Finally, after a full hour and fifteen minutes, the colonel made his decision – a Mr. Coffee from Sears value priced at $39.95.

Reflections:

° Was it wise for the colonel to engage in the coffee-maker decision?

° Why did the colonel act as he did?

° What type of power (if any) did the colonel have?

° Why do some leaders get excited about "coffee-maker decisions?"

° What does this story tell us about power in organizations?

(Authors' Reflections on page 59)

THE POWER OF NO

"NO!"

"I said...clean your room!"

"NO! You can't make me!"

"CLEAN...YOUR...ROOM! NOW!"

"NO!"

* * * * * * * * * *

Sam stared at the sheet of paper in front of him in disbelief. The document made official the fact that his contract would not be renewed the following year. He was exhausted, worn out and numb. The company he loved was getting rid of him and there wasn't anything he could do about it. The fact that he was already snatched up by his company's competitor at a substantially higher salary, didn't do much to ease his pain and confusion.

"What happened?", he wondered. He read the justification for renewing his contract that his divisional manager put forward. It was good. It contained seven solid reasons for renewal, but the Vice-President for Human Resources rejected it the same day he received it. *"Was something missing? The VP was a smart guy. Was he operating at a higher level? He must be. Something just had to be missing. What was it?"*

Sam went to speak to his division manager. It turns out he was just as puzzled as Sam. After a couple of weeks, he came to Sam and said *"I think we did miss something, Sam, but it's not what you think. We really had a rock-solid justification. Our proposal made great business sense. Period. What we missed was the 'Power of No.' Think about it, when the vice-president rejected our plan, he had us all questioning ourselves. Sure, many of us outwardly lashed out at him and questioned his ability to lead, but when we take a step back and look at the situation, we really had begun to question ourselves.*

Being a senior executive in our company, he earns hundreds of thousands of dollars a year, he is highly educated and was promoted to his current position based on merit. It makes perfect sense for us to assume that he is right and we are wrong even when all the evidence suggests otherwise. As we question ourselves, his power over us grows. And there's more. There's also a primitive, tribal aspect to this. 'No' has power. When he said 'no' to our extremely well thought out and articulated plan, he exerted his control over us. He let us know in every fiber of our being that he is dominant and in charge. 'Yes' has no such power. Think about it."

"You've got to be kidding me!", exclaimed Sam in frustration. *"Do you mean to tell me that I'm losing my job because of some elaborate power scheme whipped up by a power-crazed executive?"*

"No, Sam," replied the divisional manager. *"I don't think he whipped it up consciously. Who knows, maybe it's a habit he picked up as a kid."*

Reflections:

° What is it that gives the word "no" power?

° Why does the word "yes" lack the same power?

° Which is easier to say, "yes" or "no"? Why?

° Which word is more powerful over the long-term? Why?

(Authors' Reflections on page 60)

POWER PLAY

It was an amazing sight to see. Tony, the short-tempered, 235-pound former college football player, complete with a shaved head and a tattoo on his forearm, was getting emotional as he told his story to the seminar group. He was a low-level manager in a large manufacturing plant and was having problems with his computer. The computer technicians were swamped as their company was migrating over to a new server, but he needed help. In the past, he was always forced to drop off his laptop at the help desk and would get a call when it was fixed, often after a day or two. Once, desperately not wanting to wait two days to reinstall a program that was malfunctioning, he raised his voice and tried to intimidate the overweight and under-motivated support technician. A lot of good that did. That turned out to be a three-day job. It turned out they had to reformat his hard drive. Twice. *Yeah, right.* This time, Tony wasn't about to make the same mistake.

Being a reflective man, Tony came up with a plan. In his own words, he decided "to just suck it up." And that is exactly what he did. He walked into the tech support office with hunched over shoulders and tried to be as unimposing as humanly possible for his enormous physique. He filled out the work order form and handed it to the guy.

"I told him that it would be great to get the computer back as soon as I could. I then told him that I was on break and was heading for the coffee shop. I asked him what he liked with his coffee. I brought him back a mocha and a couple of donuts. My computer was ready for pick-up an hour later."

The group members were smiling and nodding as Tony finished his story. But Tony apparently wasn't finished. He was getting a bit red in the face when he said, *"You know, doing that was totally out of character for me. All I really wanted to do was reach over the counter and slug him, but I needed him more than he needed me."*

Reflections:

- ° Who are you dependent upon in your organization?

- ° Who depends on you?

- ° What does dependency have to do with power?

- ° How do people create dependencies in organizations?

- ° To what extent does emotion affect someone's power?

- ° What could you do to gain more power and influence in your organization?

(Authors' Reflections on page 60)

THE POWER OF KNOW

The smartest guy on the planet got off the elevator with twenty other people and walked to his office with his sack lunch. He got his Ph.D. from an Ivy League school in just three years. As part of his graduate studies, he consulted with a Fortune 100 company to improve efficiency within their transportation system. The results of his efforts made national news.

He wrote a computer algorithm that helped the company determine what plane a particular package should go on, when that plane should depart and where the plane should go. The *Wall Street Journal* reported that his algorithm will save the company $1.8 billion over a ten-year period. His algorithm provided such efficient logistics, the company decided it could operate with fewer aircraft and canceled future aircraft orders.

The great news for us is he decided not to protect his algorithm with copyrights or patents. It is available for use by us all. The bad news is the algorithm is so incredibly complex, there are only a few people on the planet who can understand it well enough to put it to good use. But they could also write a similar program if they wanted to, so a patent would really do no good.

If you were to call him the smartest guy on the planet, he'd deny it, but concede that he's pretty good at a few very specific things. He'd then say, *"We're all pretty good at something."*

Reflections:

- ° Do you have "the power of know?"
- ° In what ways are you an expert?
- ° How is your skill set unique?
- ° What could you be the best at in your organization?

° What additional influence might you have if you became an expert at something new?

° What additional power would you have if you became known as an expert at something new?

(Authors' Reflections on page 61)

LIEUTENANT THE GREAT

The young lieutenant had just graduated from college and was eager to test his leadership skills. He'd chosen a career field that allowed him to do just that, law enforcement in the military. At only 22 years of age, he was in charge of a group of 44 people ranging in age from 17 to 40. For some, this was their first military assignment. Others had more than twenty years of experience, but experience didn't matter. Rank mattered. He was the lieutenant and he outranked everyone else. This was just the way his organization was structured, and he liked it.

In addition to the wide range of age and experience, there was also a tremendous variation in attitudes among the troops. Some were living, breathing testaments to baseball, hot dogs, and apple pie. These soldiers were proud American patriots serving their country. Others were just there. They joined the military to see the world and get an education. They did their job but were pretty apathetic towards it. They certainly didn't go the extra mile or extra foot for that matter. And then there were the "stop-losses." These were the troops that wanted to get out, but couldn't. The military prevented them from separating due to global security needs and manpower shortages. Many of them lost the jobs that were waiting for them on the outside when the military wouldn't let them leave. They usually did as they were told, but they weren't exactly a happy group.

In this military organization, the first opportunity during a shift to exert one's leadership was at "Guard Mount." Guard Mount was the formal gathering of a police force before the start of a shift where new policies are briefed and inspections are conducted by the ranking cop, usually a lieutenant or junior captain. Personnel inspections were mandated by regulation and were to occur at least once in a six-day cycle.

During one of the lieutenant's first Guard Mount personnel inspections, he approached a young soldier named Smith. Smith was one of the stop-losses and his boots were atrocious. Not only was there no polish on them, but also the black leather had been worn down to gray. The lieutenant told Smith that this was unacceptable and that his boots needed to be polished by tomorrow's shift. It was clear by the soldier's facial expression that he wasn't happy and that he also wasn't taking the order seriously. After all, what was the lieutenant going to do to him, kick him out of the military? He wanted nothing more than to leave, but that was precisely the point – they wouldn't let him go. Anyway, the lieutenant thought that this was going to be a good test of his effectiveness as a leader. If he could get Smith to do what he was told, he'd consider himself pretty darn good at a pretty darn young age. As part of accepted practice, the lieutenant discussed the issue with Smith's supervisor, a highly motivated sergeant.

The next day Smith's boots looked good. They weren't great, but were more than acceptable. The lieutenant thought, *"I'm damn good. I'm young, but I've earned the respect of the troops. Many people spend their whole lives trying to become the leader that I already am."* Before he started thinking about a Presidential bid, he noticed that Smith's uniform wasn't ironed and said, *"Good job with your boots, but your uniform needs ironing."* The soldier responded, *"Yes, sir. It'll be ironed tomorrow."* And it was.

The lieutenant started comparing himself with other great leaders: Marshall, Lincoln, Churchill. Yes, they were all great, but were they great at such a young age? The lieutenant wasn't a history buff, so he didn't know for sure, but he guessed that they weren't. America was fortunate to have him on her side.

One day, while the lieutenant was out checking on the troops, he started a conversation with Smith's supervisor. They discussed the soldier's new attitude and his willingness to follow orders from the lieutenant when the supervisor looked like he wanted to say something but wasn't sure if he should. The lieutenant, an ace student of human behavior, noticed this and encouraged the supervisor to speak.

"*Well, sir, after you mentioned to me that you were upset with Smith's boots, I had a little chat with him. You see, Smith is upset with the military for not letting him leave. He really hates his job now because of it and it's hard to get him motivated.*"

The lieutenant responded, "*He's listening to me now. He just needed a leader that was willing to stand firm.*"

The sergeant looked down and said, "*Actually, Smith has been getting a little extra motivation lately. Once you told me that Smith needed to get his boots shined and that, as his supervisor, I am ultimately responsible for his behavior, I had a little talk with him. I said:*

> '*Smith, I like you. But when the lieutenant says that you need to keep your boots polished and you don't do it, well, it makes me look bad. So here's the deal. You can either do whatever the lieutenant tells you to do or I'll do everything in my power to keep you in the military as long as I can. I'll make it my personal goal to make you a "lifer" by getting you promoted ahead of your peers. I'll start by recommending you to be a shift supervisor.*'"

Reflections:

- ° What motivates the people you work with?

- ° How do you know?

- ° What does it really take for a leader to effectively motivate others?

(Authors' Reflections on page 62)

WHERE'S THE POWER?

Power...the ability to do or act to get something done. When applied to a leader, it refers to influencing the behavior of others to achieve a shared goal. It's an incredibly important topic.

When you read through the *Power* stories did you notice how each of them addressed dependencies? When leaders think of power, of how to gain it, control it and use it, they must consider the myriad of dependent relationships embedded in their organizations.

On one level, the relationship between power and dependencies is easy to understand. For example, employees are dependent on an employer for a paycheck. The leader of the organization can get dependent employees to behave in a manner others who do not covet a paycheck would not. The leader has *more power* over those who are *more dependent*. As a less obvious example, take *The Guru* story. A dependent relationship had been created between the Guru and his disciples. The Guru could not be the Guru without disciples; therefore, he was dependent on them. In this regard, the disciples have some power over him. The disciples were looking for meaning, *a Truth*, a sense of certainty they could not find on their own, so they were dependent on the Guru for those intangible elements of their lives. It is important to understand how dependent relationship can become so powerful that disciples are willing to give up their own individualism for the sense of meaning and purpose a perceived expert provides.

The power others have over us is nothing more than a function of desire. By strongly desiring a relationship with someone, we often grant him or her the power to influence us. In this sense, power is not a possession, but rather our own compliance given onto someone else. Power is created by virtue of need. It is exchange within a relationship between the "needy" and the "provider." Make no mistake about it, power is about dependencies.

When we first recognized power as a function of dependencies created by the leader, we did not realize how profound it was. Truth be told, we really didn't realize what we had discovered until we started using the concept with our clients. It's a bit like what happens on popular TV crime shows where the investigators walk into an immaculate hotel room, flip on a forensic UV light and, suddenly, the room is covered with massive blood stains. Seeing an organization through the lens of dependencies is often just as dramatic.

Power is probably best described as an imbalance in a relationship. As a function of the imbalance, one individual in the relationship has more leverage than the other. From the perspective of the leader, it provides a framework to better understand the complexities of relationships created within an organization between, well, everything.

Don't take our word for it, judge for yourself. Consider every relationship you have and think about it in terms of dependencies. Strong relationships have strong dependencies, weak ones have weak dependencies.

How do you increase your power within an organization or relationship? You increase the dependencies others have on you or decrease the dependencies you have on others. It's really quite simple, but, of course, actually putting this knowledge to work for you is a bit more complicated.

Consider this as we continue on the journey into the remaining sections. Power is the basis of control, but in order to use it effectively we need to have a broad understanding of what motivates the people who work in our organizations.

So, where's the power in your organization?

AUTHORS' REFLECTIONS...*On Power*

The Guru (p.40)

Although we could embark on a discussion about the power of charismatic leadership, doing so might not sufficiently highlight the importance of the inherent human need to be connected to others and to find purpose in our lives. Humans are meaning-seeking creatures that need to feel there is something greater than themselves. There are people who can help us find this meaning and greatness. Although The Guru is in fact a true story, it can also serve as a metaphor for a charismatic leader with a great vision in an organization. This can be a double-edged sword since we can be compelled to follow the leader to great success or disastrous failure. We can easily be blinded by our need to believe in both the vision and the leader.

If you query people who consider themselves to be astute observers of leadership, many will tell you charisma is one of the most important aspects of leadership. Despite whether or not you believe leadership exists, it is hard to deny that leaders do exist, and those who are most notable in history are often times the most charismatic. *What is it about charisma that seems to make them effective?*

The unidimensionally charismatic leader is often forgiven for not having any sort of expertise and blindly followed because they appeal to human emotion. These charismatic leaders make us feel good, and there is nothing wrong with that. But we should always be extra cautious of leaders who use charisma to gain popular support.

When people are asked to name some of the most notorious "charismatic leaders," the names of Mussolini, Hitler and Jim Jones are routinely mentioned. Looking at just this list is telling: we have to be careful not to be sucked into the power of charisma.

Laying Down the Law (p.42)

In our consulting work, we discovered an interesting phenomenon regarding the use of rules. Rules and procedures help organizations greatly by dictating how best to accomplish work and keep employee behavior within certain boundaries. Without rules, policies, and procedures, employees would have to invent their own ways of doing things which may not be efficient. People in organizations without rules would have a hard time learning since rules and policies are created from past experiences. Clearly, rules are good.

But rules taken to the extreme have a dark side. The more rules an organization has, the less discretionary power the leaders have. They can end up being bound and paralyzed by the rules they helped create.

The *Laying Down the Law* story also gets at the different types of employees which exist in organizations depicted in the chart below comparing one's actions to their intentions. *Action* refers to a person's behavior as being either compliant (obedient) or noncompliant (disobedient) relative to organizational rules, whereas *Intention* speaks to a person's desire as being either well-intended (benevolent) or ill-intended (malicious) as viewed from the organization's desired expectation of employee behavior.

	Action	
Intention	Benevolent Obedience	Benevolent Disobedience
	Malicious Obedience	Malicious Disobedience

The heroes of every organization are the *Benevolent Obedient* employees. They genuinely care about the company and follow all of the rules. Every company wants as many of these employees as it can get. The *Malicious Disobedient* employees don't survive long. They are antagonistic to the company and do not follow company rules. They are either fired or soon quit. The *Benevolent Disobedient* employees care about the company but tend to do things their own way. They push the boundaries of the organization and can instigate change. Every company needs some *Benevolent Disobedient* employees if it wants to change and grow. Finally, there are the *Malicious Obedient* employees. In the story, Chuck was a classic example of a *Malicious Obedient* employee. He didn't care about the organization, but followed all of the rules. A company is in trouble if it has too many "Chucks," especially if they are informal leaders. Unfortunately, as the story suggests, they are hard to get rid of since they tend to follow the rules.

The Coffee Maker (p.44)

Choosing the "correct" coffee-maker may very well be the first decision out of many more that will guide this organization to mediocrity, or worse. By feeling the need to exercise his power and being smart enough to know "*if it ain't broke, don't fix it*," the colonel is heading down a path of increasing triviality. As his fixation on trivial processes increases, he will siphon away the time his staff would otherwise have had to maintain the critical processes. The colonel will likely find metrics to measure the trivial concerns that he has adopted and as the old saying goes, "What gets measured, gets rewarded, and what gets rewarded, gets done."

So much of what we do is out of habit. A lot of our habits are good. We cleanse our bodies, brush our teeth, exercise, and eat (hopefully) a nutritious diet out of habit. Over time, our habits form intuitions which help lead us to good decisions. Our habits make us more efficient. We don't have to spend time thinking about holding our steering wheel in the ten o'clock and two o'clock positions, keeping our eyes on the road and our foot on the gas pedal in order to drive.

But sometimes our habits create problems for us. This usually occurs when a habit is activated out of context. In this story, we see how asking permission to buy a coffee maker activates a decision-making habit out of context. This occurs all the time, but we usually fail to see and understand what is happening. Perhaps we have a habit of unconsciousness?

Leaders will find a way to exercise their power, but they have to be mindful that power can be lost if exercised by forcing subordinates through unnecessary processes. Sometimes, the truest display of power may be *having it* but deliberately *not using it*.

The Power of No (p.46)

We see this all the time. *No* has power. Watch it in your office. Pay particular attention to what happens during meetings. When the boss is asked to make a decision and she waffles, her power and our respect for her is diminished. When the boss agrees with our suggestions, we question, ever so slightly, whether she has all the facts or if we somehow oversold her. Again, her credibility and power is diminished even if only by a fraction. But when the boss says "*no*," there is power there. She is exerting dominance, standing alone and above everyone else.

Although hearing "*no*" from an authority figure is often unwelcome, it can result in levels of motivation and commitment that might not otherwise emerge from more encouraging and validating words. Helen Keller, Sir Edmund Hillary and Jackie Robinson were told "*no*" during much of their lives. Yet today, we know their names and of their unparalleled accomplishments. But does it really matter whether any remarkable individual is told *yes* or *no*? Perhaps *no* isn't as powerful as we might imagine, unless of course, we allow it to be.

Power Play (p.48)

Tony had a lesson in power, particularly the power of dependencies. He was dependent on the computer technician who had a lot of expert power. Although the tech support guy may have had expert power, it is the dependency created in the organizational structure where most of the power lies. As we see it, the technician also had immense power to reward and coerce by withholding his services.

Tony had all of the cards stacked against him. His emotional state was a mere product of his frustration of wanting to punch the other guy. *Would this do any good?* It may if Tony elected to use coercive power in the situation. To the extent Tony adopts a primitive, tribal approach, he could hurt the technician. By doing so he could create a dependency with the Help Desk guy to serve Tony first, or be beaten. But such is the reason why laws and rules are in place. Organizations intentionally empower Help Desk personnel with the power they need to effectively and appropriately function to meet their assigned responsibilities. They are specifically designed to nullify any coercive power others might have.

Most everyone understands the basic management lesson of giving positive feedback for good work. *Why?* Because it works. If there is a law in the universe governing organizational behavior, it is probably the irrefutable fact that nearly everyone likes to be rewarded. And yet, it is not uncommon for leaders to periodically forget this.

Think about it from the Help Desk technician's perspective. Are you more likely to expedite the red-in-the-face Tony or the donut-bearing Tony? In the end, a smile and a "*thank you*" is probably the best way to leverage any power you might have.

The Power of Know (p.50)

A common first reaction to this story is, "*Good for him, but I'm not a genius and never will be one.*" Yet, *The Power of Know* story reminds us that we don't have to be the smartest person in the room to add value to our organization. Every human being is unique and capable of doing something better than others. As a leader, it's important for you to get to know your people in order to figure out where the special talents lie in each person so that you can help put those talents to good use for the organization. Everyone has the power to become and expert, and with expertise comes power.

Possessing great knowledge can be a highly-valued asset, but just as important as having relevant knowledge, a hallmark of expertise derives from the expert recognizing that which he *does not* know in order to define the boundaries of his knowledge. To the extent someone, no matter how intelligent or well-trained, truly believes everyone has the capability to be great at something, then it is quite likely he has great knowledge himself.

Lieutenant the Great (p.52)

A CEO once told us he never tells jokes outside of his company. He says he's the funniest guy in the office but falls flat with other audiences. We're sure his personnel will tell him he's also good looking, extremely intelligent and the best boss they've ever had. It seems as if leaders are often the last to know about what is really going on in their organizations. Their egos are continuously fed by almost everyone in the organization that has something to gain from a good relationship or something to fear from a bad relationship with the boss.

Consider the following thought experiment. Without reading ahead, we want you to classify the following as either *above average*, *average* or *below average*.

> 1. *What kind of driver are you?*
>
> 2. *If you have kids, how do your kids compare to all other kids their age?* (If you don't have kids, consider the question from your parents' perspective.)
>
> 3. *What kind of leader are you?* (If you have never supervised anyone, then imagine what kind of supervisor you would be as compared to your peers.)

Good. Now ask everyone around you the same questions. What do you discover? Do you see a pattern?

Finally, ask all the leaders you know to rate their abilities. The data may surprise you as it does most people who do this for the first time. The realization: How is it that most people are above average, very few are average and almost no one is below average? This is an interesting statistical distribution which speaks volumes to the astute observer.

This thought experiment helps us better understand the illusion faced by many leaders. But not just leaders, it's everyone. When people judge themselves from their own perspective, of course they are going to believe that they are as good as or better than everyone else because they are judging themselves by the same criteria by which they chose to rationalize their behavior. Leaders must constantly look at themselves from the viewpoint their followers see them. Remember, if leadership is a function of creating dependencies in followers, the more positive a follower judges you as a leader, the more effective you will be to influence his behavior. Really, your own self-perception is irrelevant. It is those who you wish to influence who matter the most.

If you ever catch yourself being self-congratulatory about what a great job you are doing as a leader, pause for a moment and consider "*why am I talking to myself?*", and then ponder why you feel the need to pat yourself on the back? Remember, the exceptional leader constantly reflects upon how she might have acted differently to evoke a more effective response from those who look to her for guidance. At the moment leadership takes a self-focused perspective, beware. Delusion lurks.

A JOURNEY INTO HUMAN NATURE

"Chains of habit are too light to be felt until they are too heavy to be broken."
—*Warren Buffett*

"We shall not cease from exploration, And the end of all our exploring, Will be to arrive where we started, And know the place for the first time."

—*T.S. Eliot*

"As I grow older, I pay less attention to what men say. I just watch what they do."
—*Andrew Carnegie*

"You cannot escape the responsibility of tomorrow by evading it today."
—*Abraham Lincoln*

"Aerodynamically, the bumblebee shouldn't be able to fly, but the bumblebee doesn't know it so it goes on flying anyway."
—*Mary Kay Ash*

MEDIOCRE FREE

Alex sat looking across his mahogany desk at a breathtaking view of the city. He had been "mediocre free" for longer than he could remember.

Many alcoholics overcome their dependency on alcohol with professional help. Social support groups like *Alcoholics Anonymous* (AA) really work. Unfortunately, no such support group exists for people who have become comfortably numb in their lives. For them, mediocrity is a destiny. Alex was comfortably numb until the day he decided he would start MA, *Mediocrity Anonymous*.

He thought back to how it all started. It was 9:00 a.m. on a Saturday morning when he cleared his throat and said, *"Hi, I'm Alex and I've been mediocre free for two weeks."* Fifteen other people sat in a circle with him having responded to an advertisement he put into a business journal. All of them were self-acknowledged, comfortably numb, mediocre executives – leaders of the most average kind. And they didn't like it. All of them wanted a change.

Everyone in the room looked at Alex and just stared blankly. It was uncomfortable. Then one of the executives said, *"Hi, Alex"* and started to clap. Then everyone else joined in and greeted Alex with applause.

Alex was delighted as he went on to tell the group his story. Until recently, he explained how he led a comfortable, yet thoroughly dull and mediocre life. He took no risks and his only ambition was to climb the corporate ladder at the same glacial pace as most of the people in his organization. In other words, his ambition was to be an average employee in an average organization. He didn't even realize that he was living a comfortable, mediocre life since that's what everyone else was doing. He never even considered an alternative way to live.

From his support group's experience, Alex discovered how comfort had become his vice. Comfort prevented him from succeeding as he had hoped. Comfort was addictive, and its result was mediocrity. Conformity was addictive and it also resulted in mediocre levels of performance.

Alex thought about how he used to be trapped in the routines and habits that formed his daily life. His office routine was always the same from his first cup of coffee in the morning while skimming the *Financial Times* to how he forwarded the last few e-mails to his home account before powering down his computer.

One day Alex woke up feeling as though his life was unbearable and it was his mediocrity which made it that way. He decided to quit his mediocre job and take a shot at being mediocre free, to find a passion and follow it to its end. He realized failure was a possibility, but taking such a risk would be the price he would have to pay to break free of his dependency on comfort and mediocrity.

In time, he also realized nearly everyone who knew him encouraged him to return to a mediocre existence in some fashion. But Alex was determined to remain strong. He wanted to be something so much more, and that is exactly what happened.

Alex started Mediocrity Anonymous nineteen years ago. He is now the CEO of his own company employing 40 others. If you work for Alex, enrollment in MA is required for all new employees. Alex never misses an opportunity to publicly acknowledge an individual's innovation and creativity in front of everyone. And without fail, following any congratulatory remarks or praise, Alex always asks, *"And how long have you been mediocre free?"*

Reflections:

   ° Why do we seek comfort?

   ° Has clinging to comfort ever held you back?

° Do you fear change?

° Can you avoid change?

° What can you do to help others embrace change in your organization?

° How can you help yourself deal with the constant change pervasive in our lives?

(Authors' Reflections on page 89)

MISTAKES

"What's wrong, Alice?", whispered Mike just as the team's first meeting was about to begin. *"You look nervous. Is everything okay?"*

Mike was Alice's new supervisor. She had just joined his team as a project manager. She came to him highly recommended by her previous supervisors. She was a terrific manager and had a reputation of doing great work.

Alice replied, *"I'm fine. It's just that I get really nervous when I start managing a new project. I'm afraid I'll make a mistake."*

Mike smiled. *"Relax, Alice. Mistakes are part of managing a project."*

Reflections:

- ° How do you feel about making mistakes?

- ° What makes some mistakes worse than others?

- ° Should we fear making mistakes?

- ° What is the relationship between learning and mistakes?

- ° Why do mistakes carry a negative stigma?

- ° Should leaders encourage their employees to make mistakes?

(Authors' Reflections on page 89)

CITIZEN JOE

Most people don't realize they have the freedom to decide who they want to be. They assume they just are who they are. So Joe was a bit ahead in this game of life.

Although Joe absolutely hated his job, he was also self-aware and realized that life was about choices. One of the biggest choices he had was to decide who he was going to be.

While Joe hated his current job, he tolerated it because he saw it as a stepping stone to the dream job for which he wasn't yet qualified. He figured he could coast through this job doing the bare minimum, not stressing over promotions or bonuses. He'd put up with the dull tasks, the unforgiving bureaucracy, the daily routines of working without getting much done. He'd not worry about making a good impression or impressing either his bosses or his peers. He'd get his new skill set and move on. It would be easy. "Two years and gone" for a slacker is no big deal.

One evening he was reflecting on what his professional life would be like if he actively managed his image. He decided that instead of not caring about anything or anyone in the company, he would try to care about *everything* and *everyone* at work. He would tackle the projects that no one else wanted. He would care about the culture and environment in which they all worked and spent their time. He would do all the little things that needed to be done but weren't in any job description. He would be the perfect organizational citizen.

Joe then asked himself an important question, *"How much difference in time and effort was there between being a model slacker and being a model organizational citizen?"*

As crazy as it sounded, Joe was forced to conclude that it was actually easier to be the perfect organizational citizen. Instead of being bored to tears spending six hours a day mindlessly surfing the Internet reviewing stock performances and football scores, he could actually try and succeed in having a positive impact on the organization. Instead of having a bad attitude all of the time, he could decide to be happy and share his happiness with others. Eight hours of happiness always beats eight hours of boredom. The choice became obvious.

Joe absolutely hated his job, until he chose to love it. After all, life's about choices.

Reflections:

° What kind of employee do you choose to be?

° Do you really have a choice?

° Does having a choice of "who you are" affect "who you will be?"

° Why would anybody choose to be a slacker?

° What is the difference between an average and a great employee?

(Authors' Reflections on page 91)

THE BLACK SUIT

The president of the large investment firm wasn't looking forward to the next interview. He'd conducted seven interviews in the last three days. He was looking forward to making an offer and being done with the process. At least this would be the last interview. The firm was fortunate to be in a position to attract exceptional talent. It was important for the president to find the right person, but truth be told, all but one of the candidates would have been a great choice. It's pretty hard to pick the best of the best when they're all the best.

But some people just know how to present themselves well. It's not just a matter of spending a lot of money on designer clothing; it's about presentation. Yes, even the parsley that accompanies a steak is important. Maurice knew how to present himself. He walked into the president's office wearing an immaculate black suit that grabbed your attention. It was perfect. He had an overcoat draped over one arm and a *Wall Street Journal* under the other. He shook the president's hand and was asked to take a seat.

Maurice carefully rested his overcoat on one of the two empty seats, placed the newspaper on top of the coat and sat down. The president seriously considered offering him a job right then and there. His presentation was that good. For no other reason than not wanting to appear as if he wasn't properly scrutinizing the candidates, the president continued with the interview. It was just a formality. Maurice would be receiving a job offer that evening.

Reflections:

 ° How important are first impressions to you?

 ° How long does it take for someone to recover from a negative first impression?

° What do you think of the president's decision-making ability?

° Was the president wrong to base his decision on first impressions?

° How long does it take you to pass judgment on people?

° How long does it take others to pass judgment on you?

° Are you presenting yourself consistently with how you want to be known?

(Authors' Reflections on page 92)

THE HAPPINESS JOKE

Sarah was in a quandary. As head of human resources for a small company, she became the self-appointed happiness guru. The company president approached her one day and told her it didn't seem like everyone was as happy as they could be or should be at work. The company was doing great, end of the year bonuses were high, and the company was having a positive impact on the community as well as everyone who purchased their products. Everyone should have been waking up Friday morning wishing it were Monday. That just wasn't happening. In fact, a lot of people were complaining. There was infighting, backstabbing and lots of back-office scheming. Employees were becoming increasingly frustrated. A few people even started floating their resumés around. This was unacceptable.

Sarah learned from talking with employees that most of the unhappiness revolved around perceptions of inequity. Apparently, employees felt that there was favoritism and people just weren't being treated fairly. People complained about unfair decisions on everything from promotions to the allocation of reserved parking spaces. The company president had prided herself on really getting to know her people and making decisions based on merit informed by a lot of data. She believed she knew who her best people were and was happy to reward them properly for their performance. What did everyone else know that she didn't? Where was the unfairness that so many people were talking about?

Sarah searched long and hard for the answer and even consulted her organizational behavior textbook from graduate school. She was reminded of the research which showed that employees determine fairness by comparing the ratio of their inputs (their effort and performance) and outputs (their rewards) to those of their peers. That would be perfectly fine if it wasn't for the fact that research has also shown humans tend to overestimate their individual contributions while underestimating those of their peers.

Based on such facts, it seemed inevitable that the boss would always appear to make unfair decisions, rendering it impossible for almost anyone to be happy at work. It just wasn't fair – and probably never could be.

Reflections:

- ° Can you please everyone at work?

- ° If not, whom should you aim to please most?

- ° What does it mean to be fair?

- ° Are you treated fairly at work?

- ° If things are perceived as unfair, what can a leader do to change the perception?

(Authors' Reflections on page 93)

OBEDIENCE

On any given day, millions of employees in thousands of organizations do what they are told to do. Undoubtedly, hundreds of thousands of people engage in activities that are good for their firms' bottom lines. Most really don't give their actions much thought though. They are good employees and do what they are asked to do.

For the past decade a man had been calling restaurants pretending to be a police detective and convincing restaurant managers to strip search their employees. There were over 70 cases in 30 states that involved managers following the impersonator's demand to strip the clothes off female employees. The employees were just doing what they were told to do. On October 31, 2006, the accused was acquitted of the charges of impersonating a police officer, solicitation and sexual abuse (see Wikipedia "strip search prank call scam").

There is nothing special about any particular day. People will do what they're told to do. They just follow orders.

"I was just following orders."

Convicted Nazi war criminal Adolph Eichmann, Nuremburg Trials, 1961

Reflections:

- Why do most people follow orders so willingly?

- Do you encourage people to challenge you when you ask them to do things?

- Do most parents you know teach their children to question their authority? Should they?

- Should leaders encourage followers to question authority?

(Authors' Reflections on page 95)

THE MILLENNIAL

"Hi, I'm Sanjay. It's not that I don't trust old people, because I do. It just seems that most people over thirty are already dead. Their bodies still move, but the life has been sucked out of them. Take my last boss for example. He had a miserable existence at the company. He did completely meaningless work and a lot of it. He was a puppet, an unthinking, uncaring pawn of 'The Man'. When his boss jumped, he jumped. The guy didn't question a damn thing, blindly following anything and everything his idiotic boss told him. Then the pathetic bastard got laid off. The same exact thing happened to my dad. Are you kidding me? Do you think I'm going to live that kind of life?

Hell no! I'm smart. I've got ambition and a degree from a damn good school. I'm going to be a CEO and run my own company. I'm going to do what I want when I want. What I want is to do something meaningful and get rewarded for it. Yeah, I may not know exactly how to do everything. I'll need a bunch of good mentors as I move up in the world, but no one is going to tell me what to do and when to do it. Blindly follow orders? Yeah, right.

I'm Sanjay. Deal with it."

Reflections:

° What do you like about Sanjay?

° What don't you like?

° Would you want Sanjay working for you? Why or why not?

° How likely is it that in the coming decades, you will have to manage employees like Sanjay?

° How would you do it?

(Authors' Reflections on page 97)

THE SHADOW

Jack was a centerpiece of his small company. He had a warm personality, got along with everyone and could be counted on for a kind word when it was needed most. He knew that people thought of him in this way and he was thrilled. He believed organizations presented a perfect opportunity, sometimes a challenge, for people to love and connect with others. Organizations, he thought, were crucibles of relationships, and maintaining healthy relationships are one of the major challenges of leadership.

Although not completely alone is his beliefs, most people were glad he was there for another reason. They liked his cooperative rather than competitive nature. He was one person whom they didn't have to race up the corporate ladder. Most people thought Jack was naïve and not really fit to fight and win the battles of survival in Corporate America. They didn't realize that the relationships and connections he was building within the company had a huge impact on *their* willingness to fight the corporate battles, but that's another story.

Although Jack took pride in the fact that his coworkers all thought that he got along with everyone, it just wasn't true. There was one woman in the office that Jack couldn't stand. It drove him crazy as it was against everything he believed about himself. He felt that it was his purpose in life to like everyone, to be kind to everyone and to validate everyone. But for some reason, when it came to Jill, he just couldn't do it and he couldn't figure out why not.

Jill wasn't a bad person. She was fiercely competitive. She often seemed a bit cold. Sometimes she was mean-spirited. It was generally agreed that she wasn't a very good team player either. So what? This describes most people some of the time and everyone part of the time.

There was one other characteristic Jack noticed about Jill. She did her best to pretend that she was the opposite of the things just described. She always greeted others with a warm smile and talked of teamwork and caring about the people in the organization. In short, she was a phony.

It just infuriated Jack. That was it. He hated the fact she was pretending to be something that she wasn't. There were a few other people in the company that felt the same way as Jack did about Jill. They were the ones who shared his philosophy about organizations being about relationships and connecting with fellow human beings. They believed in nurturing rather than hurting people. They hated confrontation and, above all, they hated fake, mean-spirited people because they could destroy all that was good in an organization.

One night, Jack woke up suddenly and came to two realizations. First, he recognized his level of anger and resentment towards Jill didn't match her crime. She really wasn't that bad. Second, he realized his anger and resentment was directed at the wrong person. He realized that just beneath the surface, *he was Jill. Holy crap!*

Reflections:

° Is there someone in your organization whom you just can't stand to be around?

° What is it that causes you to feel this way?

° Look closely just below the surface of your personality. Do you have those same traits?

° How well do you know yourself?

° To what extent might your effectiveness be limited if you refuse to acknowledge your inner motivations and emotions?

(Authors' Reflections on page 99)

RESPONSIBILITY

The boss was furious with his team. A miscommunication had occurred and something that he expected to have been accomplished hadn't even been started yet. *"What happened?"*, he asked.

There was silence for a moment as everyone did their best to avoid eye contact without appearing to do it intentionally. The truth was that the boss screwed up. He never communicated that this was a genuine tasking, let alone a priority. Now the boss was looking for a scapegoat. Everyone felt the pressure in the room weighing them down.

As everyone continued to look away, Brian, a junior mid-level manager spoke up, *"It's my fault. I'm sorry. It'll be on your desk tomorrow."*

Everyone looked up. The tension in the room vanished.

Reflections:

- ° Why might you take the blame for something that wasn't your fault?

- ° What would happen if you made it a habit to take on more blame in your organization?

- ° How can taking blame help your organization?

- ° How can taking blame help you personally?

- ° Why do you limit how you respond?

- ° Are you responsible (*response-able*) for *anything* that happens in your organization?

- ° Aren't you responsible (*response-able*) for *everything* that happens in your organization?

(Authors' Reflections on page 100)

WHAT DRIVES BEHAVIOR?

Life's about choices. We make a choice every day as to whether or not to get out of bed. We make a choice as to what we eat, where we eat it and when. When our boss or spouse does something we don't like, we usually make a choice *not* to say anything. Even as we drive to work, we make a choice whether or not we stop for coffee on the way, and if we do whether it's going to be a mocha latté or vanilla bean cappuccino.

Why? Why do we make the choices we do?

The answer is really quite simple. We tend to make choices that are good for us. Sure, we might choose to eat too much, drive too fast or do something which may appear to others as a "bad choice," but when we make the choices we do, it is usually because we expect the choice will make us feel good. Perhaps the gratifying feelings will be immediate, or perhaps they will be delayed. But regardless, we are selfish beings.

Does altruism – action for the benefit of others yielding no benefit to ourselves – *really exist?* The person who gives money to a charity anonymously can be said to be acting selfishly to the extent he feels good about himself for what he has done. Basically, people are selfish junkies always making choices which benefit themselves in some way. But this doesn't necessarily mean in doing things which are good for us, they can't also be good for other people. Quite the contrary – there are certainly levels of *good* and *bad* selfishness. Selfishness is commonly regarded as *bad* when acts have negative impacts on others.

However, there is also *good* selfishness – those acts where "all boats rise." Everyone is better off, even person who is acting selfishly. Adam Smith, the famed 18th Century economist recognized the importance of selfishness in writing *"for the butcher and baker pursuing their own self-interests, the economy works as if by an invisible hand."[1]* Yes, the American version of capitalism works because bakers are good at baking bread. They profit by their actions. The baker, in turn, can use his profits to buy shoes from the cobbler. The cobbler makes shoes because he can do it well and can also earn a profit with which, in turn, he can buy bread. All artisans and merchants perform acts at which they are skilled. Selfishly, they benefit, but in pursuing their selfishness, so do others.

What does all of this mean? Leaders need to understand the effect incentives have on behavior. Once you discover what motivates people, the calculus is really quite simple: incentives drive choices, choices have consequences and consequences drive behavior. That's it. If you want to predict how someone might behave in the future, you need to understand what motivates him. Ultimately, *incentives drive behavior.*

There are a couple of games we like to play with clients during seminars to illustrate "rational behavior." One of the favorites is commonly referred to as *The Beauty Contest Game.*[2] It works like this. Everybody is asked to (silently) choose a number from 0 to 100 and write it down on a piece of paper. The "winner" of the game is the person whose number is closest to 70% of the average of all numbers chosen. Pause for a moment and consider how you would play this game. The rules are summarized below:

(1) All participants are to choose a number from 0 to 100.

(2) Once everyone has chosen their number, *the average of all numbers chosen* is computed.

(3) This computed average is then multiplied by 0.7 (or simply, 70% of the average).

Whoever is closest to this number (70% of the average of all numbers chosen) wins!

To fully appreciate the aspects of human behavior this game brings out, you must also consider two essential questions:

> What number *would* you choose (and why)?
>
> What number *should* you choose (and why)?

Once you have thought about how you might behave, there are two other points to consider:

> Would you *really* play the game as you believe you would right now?
>
> Instead of just being played "for fun," what if the winner of the game won a $100 in cash? Would that change your behavior?

The key aspect of this exercise is a focus on how the rules of the game affect behavior. The results of this game are very predictable, and at the end of this discussion, hopefully you will understand why.

"OK, so what number did you choose?" This is how we always begin unpacking the exercise. We go around the room and have people announce their numbers. Below is a list of numbers that were actually chosen in a recent seminar:

> 66, 12, 35, 50, 25, 1, 77, 99, 28, 14, 35, 8, 0, 4

After all of the numbers have been written on the whiteboard, we start asking individual participants to explain to everyone else why they choose the number they did. Below are some actual comments:

> *"I chose 77 because it is my lucky number."*
> *"My birthday is on the 14th."*
> *"I chose 50 because it was in the middle."*
> *"I had a '66 Chevy in high school – man that was a cool car."*

And then we begin to inquire about a few numbers which always seem to come up, specifically:

> *Question: Why did you choose 50?*
> Answer: *"Well, I figured if everyone chose random-ly, 50 would be the average."*

> *Question: Why did you choose 35?*
> Answer: *"Well, I figured if everyone chose random-ly, the average number would be 50. Since 70% of 50 is 35, that should be the winning number."*

> *Question: Why did you choose 25?*
> Answer: *"Well, I figured if everyone chose randomly, the average number would be 50. Since 70% of 50 is 35, most people would choose 35. So if everyone chooses 35, the average would be 35. And since 70% of 35 is 25, that is what I chose."*

> *Question: Why did you choose 1?*
> Answer: *"Well, I just had a feeling everybody would keep trying to guess lower than everyone else, so I figured I'd have a pretty good shot with 1."*

Then, of course, there are always the outliers. These are numbers that could *never* win. Even if everybody chose 100, the average would be 100 and thus, 70% of the average would be 70. In no case could a number greater than 70 ever win the game. In this example, we had already ascertained why one person chose 77 – his lucky number. We asked the person who chose 99 what his justification had been and he replied with a wry smile on his face, *"I just wanted to keep things interesting."* Wow. And we thought these people would be trying to choose numbers which would "win" the game. How silly of us. We *assumed* the objective of the game was to win. Surprise.

It turns out in this particular demonstration, the average number was 32.4, which also brings out another interesting aspect. We have played this game with hundreds and hundreds of people over the years and only in very rare cases will someone choose a number containing a decimal. Nearly everyone chooses whole numbers. When we point this out and ask why they chose a whole number (as opposed to a mixed number with a decimal), we typically receive one of two answers. The first: *"I didn't think of that."* The other: *"We were allowed to do that?"* The point should not be underestimated. We make assumptions all the time, and most of the time we are unaware of doing so. It is both natural and essential to continually make assumptions in an effort to minimize the apparent ambiguity and complexity of problems we face. We could never navigate the complexities of life without making assumptions. The act of making assumptions is an adaptive mechanism everyone employs allowing us to merely make it through each day.

"OK, so what number **should** *you choose?"*

The average person in a seminar would typically indicate how it really doesn't matter because there is never any way to know what other people are going to do. Thus, there is no "right answer" to this game. But as it turns out, this isn't exactly correct. In fact, there is a correct answer to this game. It is a unique solution where *everybody wins*! Did you figure it out? Don't feel bad if you didn't. Only about 1 in 500 people typically see it right away. The answer: *Choose zero.*

Imagine if everyone chooses zero. The average is zero. Seventy percent of the zero is zero, so everyone wins. And yet, *zero never wins. Why?*

When you put twenty people together, zero will win only if every single person has the same perception of the game and then acts to maximize their potential gains. Such singularity of perspective with a group of individuals is rarely observed in daily life, particularly in the organizational realm. Thus, zero never wins. And if you know this, zero could never be a rational choice. It might be rational to you, but if it isn't rational to me, and my decision impacts yours, it can no longer be rational to you – even if you thought it was.

"So what is a rational choice?"

When we are making our choices, we have to consider not only what our number will be, but what everybody else is assuming our number will be. But wait, there go the assumptions again. We assume other people are playing the game to "win" (our criteria). So does the act of choosing 77 imply an irrational decision? Probably not.

Clearly, picking 77 can never be a winning choice, but this is not to suggest that such might not be a rational choice. It might only seem irrational from *our* perspective. Was the objective of the game to win, or to have fun? In this case, both. Different perspectives (*i.e.*, criteria for choice selection) lead to very different choices. To the extent you might assume the objective of the game was to win, then perhaps 77 would be irrational for *you*. But one must seek to understand the decision criteria of the person who chooses his lucky number, which mathematically can never win the game. When you dig deep enough, you will discover his primary objective was to have fun, be the "class clown" or just "mess with everybody." If indeed these are the criteria being used to "maximize satisfaction," then choosing any number, even 100, would be rational. And then there are the people who just want to be doing something else. Perhaps Walter believes it might require too much cognitive effort to think of what the "right" number would be, so he chooses 10. *Why?* It was the first number that came to his mind. *Cost?* None. *Benefit?* *"I have my number. What's for lunch?"*

Economists claim a person is rational to the extent they are utility maximizers. Meaning, individuals are deemed rational when they make choices where the benefits exceed the costs where satisfaction is maximized. Yes, people are selfish. At least this is a common assumption of economists. What isn't quite so clear is what things are considered costly and what things are considered beneficial. Be careful. Your costs might be my benefits.

"What if we change the game?"

Imagine that instead of playing "for fun," this game was played for money. Truth be told, this particular game has been widely studied by behavioral researchers, and often for money. Do results differ if this game is played for money instead of being played just for fun?

Yes, and without the deep academic explanations, the reason for observing differences in behavior is simple: incentives matter. When we play this game for money ($20, $50 or $100), the results are quite different. Instead of the "winning number" hovering in the mid-30s, it falls. The larger the prize, typically the smaller the winning number. And yet, even when playing the game with a group for a $100 prize, zero never wins. Why?

Zero can't win thanks to everybody trying to think about how everybody else is thinking about how they are thinking about everybody else's thinking… Yes, it gets complicated very fast and we always seem to be in search of quick, simple explanations. But when dealing with human behavior, nothing is simple.

For the better part of a century, psychologists have been working diligently on theories to improve our abilities to predict human behavior. But after all these years, we still aren't any closer to understanding why someone who likes both chocolate and vanilla ice cream might choose one over the other at any moment in time. Human beings are just too complex for a model to be able to accurately predict our behavior as individuals. And then, we group ourselves together into organizations, and it is the leader's job to motivate and *lead* the group towards a goal.

If we want to increase our effectiveness as leaders, we are best advised to figure out what motivates the various groups of people we serve. There are no shortcuts. We have to get to know our people. To the extent we are able to accurately predict how other people on whom we depend will behave (employees, customers, bosses, suppliers), we will have a much better chance of coming up with plans and strategies for successful action. To the extent we are inaccurate in our predictive capabilities, controlling such behavior may be more challenging than we might expect.

AUTHORS' REFLECTIONS... *On Human Nature*

Mediocre Free (p.66)

It's so natural for us to find comfort in our daily routines. We often take the same route to work, go through the same routine of checking our voice mails and e-mails, and sit in the same seat during monthly meetings. We also have the comfort of our ideas. We filter out data that is inconsistent with our world view and often associate with colleagues and friends who hold the same general views as we do. We find excuses to do the same things over and over again rather than to innovate. Staying within our comfort zone is incredibly confining, though. Think of the great people you know, including great leaders. How much time can you imagine that each of them spent "being comfortable"?

If you ask around, many people will admit that they are afraid of the dark. But if you engage them, you will discover that no one is really afraid of the dark, but rather that which is concealed by darkness that might hurt them. Human beings are naturally averse to uncertainty. That which we cannot "see" often makes us uncomfortable.

George Bernard Shaw once compared two philosophical perspectives in terms of what is considered to be reasonable. He claimed that the reasonable man tries to adapt himself to the world whereas the unreasonable man tries to adapt the world to himself. Therefore, progress can only be made by unreasonable men.[3]

Sometimes, leaders must be unreasonable, particularly when they start to feel comfortable.

Mistakes (p.69)

Most of us do far more right than wrong. We expect to get rewarded for doing things correctly and punished when we make mistakes. But a fear of punishment or disapproval in the eyes of others often creates a powerful incentive for us to refrain from taking risks. Thus, we are less likely to make mistakes, but we are more likely to stagnate and never reach our full potential. Let's start rewarding and celebrating our mistakes. It's the only way we grow.

But what is a mistake? Generally speaking, it is a retroactive judgment attempting to make sense of some outcome. And yet, it is also a value judgment in that the outcome was undesirable. The problem here is in determining what the mistake actually is. We most often point to the outcome as the mistake. The problem with this approach is that we are evaluating an outcome at one point in time even though the decision or decisions that led to the outcome occurred at other points in time. To accurately assess *the mistake* we have to consider the context within which the choices were made.

The revolutionary adhesive used on 3M's Post-It Notes (commonly known as the "yellow sticky notes") is believed to have been developed by accident. The "not so sticky" substance turned out to be a failure from another endeavor. So we are left to wonder, was this discovery a mistake or a success? Perhaps mistakes aren't always what they appear to be.

Two prominent psychologists, Amos Tversky and Danny Kahneman, conducted a study back in the 1980s looking at pilot training in Israel.[5] They observed that when a student pilot performed very well on a particular flight, the instructor praised him. Then they observed that on the very next flight, almost inevitably, the student performed much worse. Similarly, they observed that when a student pilot performed poorly by making lots of mistakes on a test flight, he would be chastised by the instructors. The result was quite predictable – he would do far better on the next flight. The conclusion seemed obvious: punishing people for mistakes would improve performance. But it turns out, that was *exactly* the opposite of what they found. They discovered there was absolutely *no* causation between punishment and performance. Punishment had little to do with correcting future mistakes. Mistakes were simply part of the learning process. Instead, these researchers reasoned that what was really being observed was nothing more than the mathematical anomaly referred to as "regression to the mean."

What's the point of this story? Mistakes may not always be as they appear. In fact, what might be perceived as a mistake may simply be an observation of statistical variance.

Leaders must always remain mindful that if they aren't observing mistakes from their followers, it is likely that there isn't much learning occurring in the organization. Perhaps for some organizations such an observation is good, but more often than not, a lack of observed mistakes is a sign of stagnation. Of course, there are different types of mistakes. Some mistakes emerge out of negligence and may be less forgivable than others that just might occur from trying something new or taking a calculated risk. However, leaders should always be on the lookout for those mistakes that are worthy of celebration.

One final thought on mistakes. There are mistakes of omission and mistakes of commission. For some reason, mistakes made as a result of poor choices are often judged to be more forgivable than mistakes made by not acting. It is not uncommon for leaders to (mistakenly) believe that they *have* to take action because that's what leaders do! Not necessarily so. Doing nothing can be the best choice available to the leader who is aware that he can act, but he chooses not to.

Citizen Joe (p.70)

We think that the power of this story needs to be experienced. Try a little experiment. Tell yourself that for the next week you are going to love your job completely and then *"fake it 'til you make it."* Go about your job and interactions with your coworkers as if you've just landed in paradise and you have the best job with the best people in the world. Be a *Benevolent Obedient*. At first it will likely feel fake and contrived, but with a little persistence, you will likely start appreciating your job more and more. Another variation on this is to target one coworker that you dislike and imagine him or her as someone you truly value and care about. See what happens. We've tried this on many occasions and have always been amazed with the results. We truly do create our own realities.

Indeed, life is about choices, and choices have consequences. In the end, it should be the consequences driving our behavior. Most consequences are self-critiquing. When we get positive feedback from our actions, we tend to recognize that good actions generally lead to good results. However, when the feedback is something less than positive, we tend to dismiss it, or worse, blame the outcome on other factors.

Consider the consequences of Joe's previous behavior. How do you think he was treated by his co-workers, his boss, or anyone else in his organization? Then consider how he was likely treated by those same people after the behavioral change.

Famed psychologist B.F. Skinner[4] would likely tell us that the positive reinforcers that Joe experienced with his newfound behavior made where he worked a better place and made his boss and co-workers better people to Joe. The result is that Joe became dependent on the approval and liking of others and actually became the "good citizen."

The Black Suit (p.72)

We're interacting with people all the time and often do so without saying a word. Sometimes, as in a job interview or a meeting with our boss, we are very conscious of the impressions we are trying to make on others. Most of the time, however, we just default into the habit of who we are and interact without consciously thinking about who we want to be and who we want others to see. Our actions create our reality whether we like it or not and we're always on display.

If you consider the research on job interviews, the findings are disturbing. Interviews typically do very little to explain the variance in employee performance after they are hired. In fact, in some cases, selecting candidates using only an application and resumé better explained future performance than using face-to-face interviews. So one has to wonder, why do organizations continue to use interviews, particularly since they can be so costly?

Some managers would claim that they want to judge the person's "interpersonal skills" or "verbal communication skills." But what ends up getting judged at most interviews (the type with standard Q&A) is the 15-minute presentation and performance. Some very marginal candidates could come in very polished and well-prepared. Other far more superior candidates may not feel so well that day and just be off their game.

The point of this particular story is how *easy* it is to judge a book by its cover. We do it all the time without thinking about it. The exceptional leader is one who is aware of this bias and tries not to let his or her good judgment become clouded by extraneous factors. In the end, the factors used to judge others should be directly related to the knowledge, skills and attitudes necessary to perform the assigned job. Little else should matter, but invariably, it does.

Even if a candidate's knowledge, skills, and abilities (KSAs) to do a job can be ascertained from the data contained in an application package, most leaders will still opt for the interview. They want to know if a person has interpersonal skills, social astuteness, and emotional intelligence. Are they going to be emotional bricks in the organization or passionate and compassionate colleagues? Leaders opt for the interview and allow it to trump the KSAs. But think about it, how bad could a team of Maurices really be?

The Happiness Joke (p.74)

It's not a very funny joke. Unfortunately, equity issues can drive organizations into a downward spiral. It is common to overestimate our individual contributions while underestimating the contributions of others. This phenomenon tends to skew our perceptions of equity. Trust seems to be the only antidote to the *"dis-ease"* caused by perceived inequity. When employees trust their leadership implicitly, when they know that the leadership is looking out for the best interests of each employee, these perceptual difficulties disappear. Unfortunately, it's extremely difficult to reach this level of trust.

People tend to confuse *equality* and *equity* when these concepts have very little to do with each other. Equality is simple – everything is the same on the dimension of interest: same size, same weight, same amount, same value. *Equality is about a sameness.*

Equity on the other hand is a far more sophisticated concept. *Equity is a perception of fairness* in the eye of the beholder. The problem arises when there are many beholders, there may be many differing perceptions of what *fair* is. As one of our colleagues likes to put it, *"The only definition of 'fair' that we can ever really agree on is the space between the foul lines on a baseball field."* That's fair.

We like to pretend that everyone is equal, but when you give this cliché just a bit of thought, you realize how ridiculous it is if you take it as a literal notion. People are very unequal in terms of their knowledge, skills and attitudes to do a variety of jobs. So why would a leader even consider treating everyone equally? Consider as an example that you are an aviation sales representative, would you want to be treated the same way as an airline mechanic or a pilot? Mechanics must go to continuation training classes on emerging propulsion technologies while pilots must sit for hours in the flight simulator to be evaluated by their superiors. Can you imagine other people sitting through the multi-hour sales presentations that you must endure? Of course not. *We expect to be treated differently.*

But at a higher level, what we all really desire is equitable treatment. Give us the same opportunity to succeed in our jobs that you have in your job. To the extent the leader creates a climate based on trust and respect where everyone has equal opportunity, then and only then, can equity and equality be compared. We'll address this more thoroughly in *A Journey Into Control*.

Obedience (p.76)

Rules free us from thinking about routine decisions that we would have to make over and over and over again and allow us to focus our attention on non-routine tasks that are outside the scope of existing rules. However, rules can also free us from having to think at all.

We'll never know for sure if its nature or nurture, but unquestionably nurture has a tremendous influence on our desire as human beings to be obedient. We are taught to obey our parents. We are taught to obey our teachers. We are taught to obey traffic laws. And up until the mid-20th century, many women in the U.S. took marriage oaths to "obey" their husbands. Unquestionably, obedience to authority is necessary for social systems to function, but where are the limits?

Stan Milgram ran some of the most famous experiments in psychology in the early 1960s, in which ordinary people were asked to participate in research on human learning.[6] Individuals were recruited to administer electric shocks to another person in an adjoining room who was attempting to learn sequences of words. When the "learner" erred, the "teacher" administered electric shocks starting with very low voltages and escalating to what appeared to be potentially lethal levels. What the "teacher" subject did not know is that everyone was in on the experiment except him, and the research wasn't investigating learning, but rather obedience. The results were staggering. Two-thirds of the recruits were so deferent to an authority figure (an experiment supervisor wearing a white lab coat), that the experiment participants continued administering these apparent extreme electric shocks even when the "learner" screamed in pain and eventually stopped responding. Milgram's point was motivated by Nazi behavior during the Holocaust and the classic defense that *"I was just following orders."* It was one of the most powerful psychological demonstrations in the history of science.

What does this have to do with leadership? Consider the kind of environment in which your employees or co-workers operate. Are people conditioned to blindly follow rules, policies and directives, or are they taught to question authority?

We can all appreciate why parents desire that their children obey their wishes. In most cases, it keeps the children alive, safe and healthy. But as children get older, one has to question the extent to which a parent should demand obedience and instead encourage inquiry. In any developmental setting, leaders of all types should encourage their followers to be mindful before acting out of blind obedience and instead use their own minds and intuition to make decisions.

Our need to obey is based on a lifetime of socialization and is the essence of human cooperation within societies. Indeed, Freud cautioned us to not underestimate the power of the "need to obey." From our earliest years we are conditioned to obey authority, but there are also several other factors that can influence our tendency and desire to obey. First, we may perceive that the person we desire to obey is an authority figure – an authority that we respect. We may even be tricked by things such as the wearing of a uniform (or in the case of the Milgram example, a white lab coat and a clip-board). Second, we may also depend on the authority figure. As we have discussed in earlier sections of this book, if a person can satisfy a need we may have, we tend to obey their demands.

The situation in which we find ourselves could also profoundly impact our desire to obey. This is persistently evident in crisis or emergency situations. At no other time are we more inclined to defer to authority than when faced with considerable ambiguity as to how to act, or react. At such moments, we are much more likely to obey the directions of authority figures even if we are unaware of our inclination to do so. Thus, regardless of our perspective on obedience to authority, human nature is unlikely to change anytime soon. Some people have a need to be obeyed, but all of us have some level of a need to obey others, even if we deny it exists.

The Millennial (p.77)

The Millennials are coming! The Millennials are coming!

We should hear human resources managers everywhere shouting this from the roof tops of their companies. We should hear it, but we don't. We believe that the Millennials are a very powerful group of people who are just starting to make their impact on organizations. Those who believe that they will simply be indoctrinated into the workplace without incident are likely victims of old-school thinking.

The most common comment we routinely hear from senior human resource management executives is *"How do we change this generation to fit our organization?"* The answer is, *"You don't, you change the organization."* This newest generation believes they are entitled to great jobs with great benefits. Despite how arrogant such a statement might sound to you, it might be more correct than incorrect. One quick look at the labor projections over the next twenty years reveals the retirement of the Baby Boomers is forecasted to create a significant labor shortage. These bright young men and women will have plenty of choices. *Who will they choose?* We suspect that it won't be the organization that tells them they need to conform to the status quo if they have other options.

"The young people of today sure aren't the same as they were in my day. What is happening to society?" If you guessed that this was a quote from the 1920s, you'd be correct. And yet, we all hear words like this uttered in the halls of organizations today. What are we to

make of this?

Change. It is all around us. And yet the one place we find it most difficult to recognize is in the mirror. Sure, each of us might look a bit older, but in our mind's eye, do we feel any different than we did a decade ago? Not really, but we sure can recognize everything else around us that is different. And that is the problem. We have a hard time trying to change our frames of reference to not only recognize change, but rather to anticipate it. We can all detect change when it occurs, but forecasting it is much more difficult.

The best determinants of what changes are likely to manifest in the next five years can often be found by analyzing the attitudes, habits and perspectives of the twenty-somethings entering the workforce. This is our future. Leaders, nobody seems to appreciate these guys. You have the pick of the crop, if you are savvy enough to know how to find the best. Or, if you are starting to understand leadership as an art of inquiry and creation, perhaps it matters not so much for finding the right people, but instead retooling your leadership perspective to work with what you have. Here's the secret: They all have the power to be "GIANTS"! *Do you have the power within yourself to inspire them?*

Connoisseurs of leadership are usually well acquainted with Maslow and his thoughts about motivation and development.[7] Most students find his hierarchy of needs initially appealing, but soon recognize that Maslow probably only had it partially correct.

It worked in an Industrial Age where organizations were mechanistic. Production required efficiency. Baby boomers yielded a tremendous labor supply. They relied on organizations not for just a paycheck, but identity, meaning and purpose. It was about structure and hierarchy. The end game was the corner office, a window view and a reserved parking space. It was about a gold watch and a pension. People depended on organizations. The organizations had the power.

Then the transition began. A new generation was born. It was hard to define in terms of identity. In fact, they didn't even get a real name, Generation X. And then came the Millennials. These were the kids that didn't keep score when they played soccer. They were told that everyone was a winner. There didn't need to be losers. Where self-actualization used to be at the top of the Maslow pyramid, contemporary enculturation may be redefining it as a basic need. Time will tell, but it seems that the Millennials are here to stay. *Leaders, be advised.*

The Shadow (p.78)

Whenever we are angry with someone and our degree of anger exceeds that of the perceived crime, we should look within ourselves. When we scratch below the surface of our personalities, we often discover the very trait that we dislike in another is within us just waiting to be released. At some level, we all repress some aspects of our personalities. The issue becomes one of hypocrisy. Hypocrisy is often a result of a long-repressed personality trait. A great example of this we've seen in the media is when a politician promoting an anti-gay agenda is later caught engaging in homosexual acts. We can only repress aspects of our personalities for so long before they burst into the forefront.

Surely you work with someone that you really don't like. Ask yourself how much of what you don't like about them is them and how much of it is you? If you are normal, you probably believe that about 95% of the reasons for not liking that person are completely due to them. But then consider if the same question was posed to them about you. What would they say? Chances are, they would likely feel the same way about you – 95% your fault. And you know what? You are probably both right. We all are responsible for creating the social realities in which we operate, but yet we prefer to believe that there is an objective social reality that exists within our work environments and that we merely interact within it. By interacting, we are changing the nature of *all* the relationships.

The Shadow is a story about self-awareness. You may be well aware of how others might perceive you, but to what extent are you aware of how you are affecting others' behavior by how you react to what they say and do? It isn't too difficult to become as unaware as Jack (in the story) from time to time without even realizing it.

Responsibility (p.80)

To the extent that leadership is the act of creating dependencies between a leader and a follower, consider how power permeated the room when the boss spoke and again when Brian replied. The boss has legitimate power to be the leader. When he spoke, he created tension and put everyone else in a defensive posture. People naturally assume defensive postures when they feel threatened and prepare to fight back. Everyone can recognize that such an approach can be detrimental to creating a trusting relationship between leader and follower. No one wants to work for a boss like this.

Your ability to respond is crucial to enhancing your organizational power. Think about it – responsibility, or *response-able*.[8] It's interesting to play with this concept. To what are we able to respond? Is there anything to which we cannot respond? As we explore our ability to respond we realize that we are always free to respond to our situation. Our response to events is a choice that we are free to make. Of course, our responses have consequences, but we get to choose them as well.

What good is achieved by placing blame on a person? Can't we instead substitute the word "responsibility" for the word "blame"? Blaming someone might make us feel better because then we feel self-righteous. But what is the effect on all those around us? How do others perceive us after we have placed blame on someone else? Just consider how you perceive someone who is passing the buck.

We often feel the need to assign blame when decisions go awry. Why might we feel inclined to blame someone for something that we perceive to be bad, wrong or messed up? Perhaps, deep down we want to ensure that everyone else knows it wasn't our fault. *No sir, not me. It was him!* Why do we feel this way? Maybe we realize that because all the parts and pieces are related, in a complex organization, or when something goes wrong, the real "cause" might lie somewhere else. If you ever feel the need to blame someone that you work for (or worse, someone who works for you), reconsider, it can be caustic.

People want to be around leaders like Brian. Brian knows how to respond to make others feel comfortable because he takes stress and tension away from the rest of us. Brian makes us feel good because Brian is *response-able*.

A JOURNEY INTO CULTURE

"An army without culture is a dull-witted army, and a dull-witted army cannot defeat the enemy."
—*Mao Zedong*

"Giving people self-confidence is by far the most important thing that I can do. Because then they will act."
—*Jack Welch*

ASSUMPTIONS

As Celina left work, she looked across the parking lot and saw the rest of her co-workers getting into their cars. She waved, and they waved back. She knew they didn't know. Everyone makes assumptions about everything all the time. Most of the time, they aren't even aware of it.

The team had been going to the sports bar on the other side of town every Thursday night for almost a year now. All of them, except Celina. It was like having a weekly office party, minus one.

Oh sure, they knew Celina was aware of their weekly outing. They had invited her a few months ago when she let on she knew about it. After a few red faces and uncomfortable moments, everything was back to normal. She declined the forced invitation and they went back to assuming that now everything was all right. Some of them even smiled as they waved to her. Of course, she smiled and waved back.

But this office outing was the least of it. At least it only occurred once a week, and after work hours. It was the other 40 hours per week that she dreaded. It was bad enough hearing all of the vulgar language in the office all the time, but then came the gay jokes. *"You're such a homo"* or *"what a gay excuse"* were regular phrases in the office.

It's tough being the boss, especially when everyone thinks you have the easiest job in the organization.

Reflections:

° How effective do you think Celina would be as the leader of her organization?

° Imagine that Celina asked your advice as a friend as to

what she might do to improve the culture of her organization. What would you tell her?

° To what extent can a leader affect the culture of an organization?

° Suppose Celina was a recovering alcoholic, would your assumptions about her change?

° Why do we make the assumptions we do?

(Authors' Reflections on page 121)

LADIES AND GENTLEMEN

Some people are born to do what they do, and Dr. Z was born to be a business professor. He loved his students and his students loved him. He always found a way to create a nurturing and productive classroom environment no matter what challenging circumstances might be present. On top of genuinely caring for his students, he knew his subject as well as any professor could. He was the best. But it wasn't what he knew about academics that made him so effective – it's what he knew about *people*.

He understood the importance of providing a transition from outside life to the learning environment in the classroom for his students. No one ever saw it coming, and that was its beauty.

On the first day of class, he routinely selected a student with a deep radio voice to act as the announcer for the entire semester. *"From this day forward,"* he told the class, *"the announcer will give me a proper entrance greeting."* He suggested that they try it now as he walked out of the classroom. As he slowly walked in and closed the door, the announcer in a perfect talk-show voice said, *"Ladies and gentlemen…Dr. Z!"* Dr. Z, in true late-night talk-show form entered the class and started working the crowd. The class would applaud. He would continue to work the crowd, shaking a few hands, feigning surprise at the positive response from the class and wait for the crowd to quiet down.

This first day event was, to some extent, an uncomfortable act for many. The class would go through the motions and play along, but they would never take it seriously. To an outside observer, it may even appear as a spectacle which failed miserably.

Nevertheless, Dr. Z chugged along. Day after day, Dr. Z would insist that the class act in this same fashion. Some days he'd enter imitating David Letterman. Other days he'd be Conan O'Brien. There would be slight variations every day, but it was basically the same act. However, by the end of the semester, it wasn't an act anymore. The students clapped and cheered with genuine enthusiasm as Dr. Z entered class. Dr. Z had become a "star," greeting his crowd accordingly.

Semester after semester, he was among the highest-rated faculty members in the college.

Reflections:

- ° What "scripts" do you enact, consciously or unconsciously at work?

- ° Are these scripts good or bad for the organization? Why?

- ° What new scripts or routines would be beneficial for you to create?

(Authors' Reflections on page 123)

EXEMPLARS

As the ceremony began, Simon leaned back in his chair to get as comfortable as he could for the next hour. The president of the company, the city mayor and a half-dozen prominent faces from the local community sat on the platform next to Mr. Tinsley's widow. No expense had been spared for today's dedication ceremony naming the company's headquarters building, Tinsley Tower. In turn, each of the prominent leaders stood behind the microphone and addressed the crowd, attesting to the greatness of Mr. Tinsley. It seemed that no leadership adjective had been left unsaid. A casual bystander might just believe that whoever this Mr. Tinsley was, he may have been one of the greatest leaders to have ever lived.

Simon sat back and studied the faces of each of the men on the platform making the speeches and wondered if they actually believed what they said. He gazed at Mrs. Tinsley and wondered what was really behind her smiling mask. Simon knew lots of things. Simon was not only one of the founding members of the company, but he and Jim Tinsley had been college roommates. He probably knew and loved Jim more than anyone else in attendance today. But that didn't change the facts, at least not as Simon saw them. To preserve his friendship with Jim, he left the company years ago. In retrospect, it was one of the best decisions he ever made. They remained best friends until the end.

Simon knew Jim wasn't the perfect leader everyone wanted to make him out to be. He was both an alcoholic and a workaholic. He had three grown children who barely knew him. None of them bothered coming today, nor did they go to the funeral last year. Several of Jim's mistresses came, but Mrs. Tinsley pretended not to see any of them, as she had done for most of her married life. Simon was intrigued with how everyone seemed to have forgotten about the financial scandals and accusations of the early 1980s that hung like a dark cloud over Jim Tinsley. The company lost millions while the Tinsleys built their fifth home in Aspen, Colorado.

Simon guessed that none of that mattered now. This was the most extravagant ceremony he had ever seen the company put on. To hear the speeches, it was obvious that the company wanted to honor Jim Tinsley. After all, it is important to remember our leaders.

Reflections:

° Do you know what your subordinates expect of you?

° Are you willing to fulfill that role for them?

° How likely is it that you will fail to live up to subordinate expectations? How will you deal with it?

° How "human" do people expect their leaders to be?

(Authors' Reflections on page 125)

BATTERED

The phone rang and she knew it was him. She lunged for the phone in a desperate attempt to get it on the first ring. She knew he'd be angry otherwise. *"Hello,"* she said.

"It's me. Where were you?" he asked. *"I called ten minutes ago."*

"I had to step out. I was only gone a minute," she said hesitantly.

"You know I expect you to be there when I call. We'll discuss that later. Right now I want to know if you did what I asked you to do."

Her body tensed and was flooded with fear. *"Yes, but what was the last thing you wanted?"*

His voice lowered and changed its tone. It was condescending and had an unmistakable element of anger embedded within it. *"I told you what I wanted yesterday afternoon. You even asked me to repeat it and I did. I'm not going to tell you again. I'll be over in 30 minutes. For your sake, it better be good, perfect. You do remember what happened last time, right?"*

"Yes," she whispered.

He slammed the receiver down and felt the anger coursing through his blood.

She sat motionless and imagined the nightmare that awaited her. She wasn't exactly sure what would happen, but she did know that it wouldn't be good.

(There are two endings to this story)

The first ending:

The man pulls into the driveway, slams the car door shut and bursts through the front door to find his wife sobbing in the corner.

"I couldn't remember what you wanted," she cried.

"You just can't do anything right, can you!", he screams.

The second ending:

The man bursts into her office. *"Let me see the presentation slides. Now!"*

She fumbles through a pile of papers and hands him a short stack. *"I hope this is what you wanted."*

"No, no, no!" he blurts out. *"I can't believe you screwed up again. I told you exactly what I wanted. I told you twice and you still blew it. You're not leaving tonight until this is done, until it's perfect. On top of that, I need you to do something else. Do you think you can get this right?"*

She listened with instinctual intensity as her boss gave her instructions. Glancing at the many certificates on her wall commemorating 23 years of outstanding job performance, she was overcome with doubt, insecurity and fear.

Reflections:

   ° Does this story offend you? If so, why?

   ° Which type of abuse is worse, physical or emotional?

   ° To what extent does abuse affect you at work?
      (*Note: Abusive behavior need not go to extremes like above. It can be subtle ridicule. It can be a gesture, a frown or ignoring others at the office. It can be anger, frustration or a passive-aggressive smile.*)

   ° What can you do to make your coworkers and subordinates feel more comfortable at work?

(Authors' Reflections on page 126)

CREATIVITY AND DIVERSITY

It was an extremely benign and perfunctory meeting to discuss and validate the academic department's curriculum. The only decision on the table was whether or not to make a second semester of accounting mandatory for all business majors rather than the elective course it had been for the last several years.

The discussion that ensued could best be described as a choir rehearsal. Many people sang in praise of the course and how important it was to the curriculum. They, in perfect unison, sang that it should be mandatory. Others, again in perfect harmony, sang in praise of the course but said that it wasn't necessary to make it mandatory since most of the students take the course anyway.

To some extent, the diversity became a duet: praise and make the course mandatory; praise and leave the curriculum unchanged. All was good. All was harmonious. The music was beautiful. Everyone enjoyed the collegial discussion of ideas just as academicians were supposed to.

Unfortunately, one faculty member didn't quite get it. She sang out of tune. During the meeting she spoke up and said it was insane to make classes mandatory, Students should have no required classes – they should be encouraged to decide what courses are best for them based on their interests and goals for the future.

The music stopped.

Everyone at the meeting acknowledged what she said with the utmost courtesy. They thanked her for the input and even discussed the idea for a few moments. Then the idea just faded away. It was gone, never to be discussed again. A vote was held and it was decided to make the course mandatory. Alas, the music resumed once again.

The woman with the out-of-tune voice felt alone and unwelcomed. She couldn't point to any specific action or behavior which made her feel this way, but she felt out of place and disowned. The best analogy she could come up with to describe the experience was to imagine everyone else at the meeting taking turns singing as part of the choir. When it was her turn to sing, she felt as if she had instead presented them with pornography.

At one level this made no sense, yet, at another level, somehow it did.

Reflections:

- Do you have a diverse organization?

- How do you know?

- How would you describe the relationship between diversity, ideas and innovation?

- Whose voices are most important in achieving "harmony" in your "choir"?

(Authors' Reflections on page 127)

PRIMING

The CEO put the newspaper down and reflected silently for a long time. She had just read about a study conducted by some prominent psychologists that blew her mind. In the study, a lab assistant carrying textbooks, papers, a clipboard, and a cup of coffee intentionally bumped into student test subjects. When the books fell out of the lab assistant's hands, the subjects were asked to hold the cup of coffee while the assistant picked up the books. Analysis revealed that the coffee had an influence on how the subjects rated a hypothetical person later that day. If the cup of coffee the subjects held was cold, they rated the hypothetical person as colder, less social, and more selfish than the subjects that held a hot cup of coffee. Apparently, the cold cup of coffee triggered or primed the person to later access concepts dealing with "coolness." The same was true for hot coffee priming concepts dealing with "warmth."

The CEO could not stop thinking about how she unintentionally primed her employees both positively and negatively through her day-to-day actions. She wondered if when she referred to the competition as a "bunch of bastards," she primed them to judge each other negatively throughout the day or, God forbid, to treat each other as bastards. Could the mere mention of the company's "great" strategy create great employees?

Reflections:

° Is it possible *not* to prime people with whom you interact?

° How important is priming to effective leadership?

° What are some examples of effective priming in your organization?

° Do you know how to effectively prime people you work with?

° How might you use priming to help meet personal and organizational goals?

(Authors' Reflections on page 128)

THE GRAND ILLUSION

Ed sat in the back of the room watching the briefing. The slide showing diversity in the organization was up for about ten seconds. As he remembered them, the current statistics were:

- Men 67% / Women 33%

- Whites 68% / Blacks 14% / Hispanics 11% Asians 5% / Others 2%

He wondered why they even showed this slide. What meaning was it trying to convey to the audience? *"So what if you end up with all men or all whites?"* he said to himself. *"If they are the best out there, why would the organization even care?"* He knew exactly what the people in the audience were thinking.

Ed chuckled to himself. In the end, he knew perfectly well what the real story was. He should. He was the CEO. He made it a habit to occasionally sneak in the back of meetings like this just to get an idea of what message the mainstream employees were really hearing. And it was fun.

Ed wished he could show the data that really mattered:

- Fat 78% / Thin 22%
- Heterosexual 89% / Gay 6% / Bisexual 3% Asexual 2%
- Conservative 18% / Moderate 64% / Liberal 18%
- Ultra religious 14% / Somewhat religious 61% Agnostic 14% /Atheist 11%
- Intolerant 100%

Much had changed in the United States since the Civil Rights, Affirmative Action and Equal Rights movements, thanks to Congress. But the fundamental problem still remained, and it was as challenging as ever.

Reflections:

° Do you buy Ed's assessment that everyone is intolerant?

° What is the optimal level of diversity for your organization?

° How many child molesters or drug-abusers do you want working with you? Where do you draw the line on diversity?

° How do you categorize people? What are your biases? Do you judge others based on who they are or what they do? Is your discrimination justified?

° To what extent is diversity "a grand illusion?"

(Authors' Reflections on page 133)

WHY DOES CULTURE MATTER?

If leaders are guilty of making one mistake more often than any other, it is probably their misperception or misunderstanding of the nature of organizational culture. Despite their insistence to the contrary, our experience indicates most leaders don't fully understand or appreciate the culture in which they are operating.

Leaders must first come to understand what culture *is* and what it *isn't*. Notwithstanding the many definitions that have been advanced, the collective academic inquiry into the domain of organizational culture has revealed two basic aspects worth pointing out. First, culture is the emergent product of social interaction among human beings working with one another in a group with a shared goal. Culture isn't something you can easily identify. Many people think of culture in terms of the values, symbols, ceremonies and norms which manifest in the various structures, policies and attitudes of the organization. A more thorough perspective of culture recognizes it as something far larger than most would ever assume. As the "glue" of an organization, it is very often the attribute which defines the organization's collective identity. And yet, it is quite common for leaders to talk of making a "cultural shift" in their organization. We're not saying it isn't possible for a culture to change, but leaders rarely can change culture as easily as they believe they can.

Consider your own identity. What is it that makes you, *you*? Now imagine you wake up one morning and want to change who you are. After all, you are in control of *you*, right? Can you change *you* into someone else? Perhaps. But it would take the greatest of cognitive, emotional, physical and psychological efforts. Changing an organization's culture is no different. You are *you* just as an organization's culture *is* the organization.

You really need to look no further than the US Marine Corps, Mary Kay cosmetics consultants, or Tibetan monks to appreciate the importance of organizational culture. Just as civilizations across the face of the Earth are defined by their societal cultures, so too are organizations. It's almost unthinkable to imagine one could change a culture by becoming the president or prime minister of its citizens. Organizations are no different.

Probably the best metaphor for understanding the essence of cultural change is to consider how individuals change over the course of their lives. Are you the same person you were twenty years ago? How about last week? Indeed, each of us changes in response to the environments in which we find ourselves. We are adaptive beings and are very good at dealing with change, even if we don't like it. Because of our dislike for change, we resist it and entrench ourselves in that which we know and find comfortable. But often this is a short-term perspective. To the extent the environmental stimuli we encounter persist over the long-term, we typically have two choices. We can change our behavior and adapt to the changed structure of the environment or we can face the forces of natural selection.

It is worth pointing out that leaders frequently confuse the concepts of *culture* and *climate*. Despite a leader's best attempts, culture can't be changed by edict, but it can be shaped over time by making changes to policies, structure and vision. It is a long-term proposition. *Organizational climate*, however, is quite different. Climate is a snapshot perspective of the organizational environment today. Climate, unlike culture, is far easier to influence over the short-term. It doesn't take long for a leader to develop a sense of how satisfied her employees are with the work environment. Is there a sense of esprit de corps? Are employees satisfied with their immediate supervisors? Do they feel they get the support they need? Are management policies deemed to be equitable? Is performance rewarded? Do people feel a sense of accomplishment at the end of each day? These are just a few questions to consider when determining how healthy an organizational climate is – or isn't. Here's the secret: organizations which can sustain a positive climate with high levels of employee satisfaction and performance are also those that typically have highly functional organizational cultures. The connection? Leaders.

If the leader takes care of the immediate needs of the organization's climate, the long-term need to change a culture tends not to manifest. Every parent knows this. If you want to raise your child to become a responsible, trustworthy and capable adult, you can't force their identity at age eight into what you want it to be at age eighteen. Instead, you tend to their developmental needs throughout adolescence and hold them accountable to the same values that define your family. Similarly, as a leader, if you envision the future of your organization to be something different than it is today, it is your responsibility to reshape the policies, procedures and structures to create the behaviors conducive to the development of your organization and its members.

People will watch how the leader behaves to make sense out of this journey towards change. A leader creates a new reality in how she responds to a crisis, how she reacts to environmental shocks, what metrics she measures, what behaviors are rewarded and punished and whom she decides to promote, hire and fire. Over a prolonged period of time, the culture can change.

Culture change is not a destination – it is a journey. Climate change, however, is a destination. It is healthy or it isn't. To the extent the climate is positive, leaders have a much better chance of creating a shared vision of the future.

AUTHORS' REFLECTIONS...*On Culture*

Assumptions (p.104)

We tend to assume that people we like have the same beliefs and values that we do. *Why?* Research findings inform us that *people we like tend to be people like us.* What we don't know or have data on is how often the assumptions we make about others are wrong and we never become aware of our error. It's hard to estimate the damage that poor assumptions can have on an organization, but it certainly isn't trivial.

Organizational life is complex and ambiguous because we can never know what other people are thinking. We don't truly know their motivations or how they perceive the words and actions of others. It isn't so much what we don't know, but rather what we don't know we don't know.

Most effective leaders exert great effort to get to know their people. This may sounds like a cliché, because the term is overused. But regrettably, the practice isn't. Ironically, many leaders assume they know what this cliché means, and yet through their actions they demonstrate that they don't. Some leaders believe that getting to know their people means remembering family members' names, birthdays and favorite sports team. Although this is certainly a start, "getting to know your people" goes far deeper.

Let us diverge for a moment and tell you another story about a man named Paul. Paul was seemingly very similar to everyone else in his office. He tended to be agreeable and was well-liked. At a promotion party for Paul, his boss got up in front of everyone to talk about his life and career. The boss "knew" that Paul loved baseball as a kid and played second base on his community's little league team. This caught everyone by surprise as no one seemed to have known this. Perhaps it's what makes dinners like this tolerable

– you tend to learn things about people with whom you work that you might otherwise never know.

The boss continued his remarks by professing how he "knew" that Paul got his only B+ in handwriting in third grade and joked about how much he now loved his Blackberry. Everyone laughed. He also "*knew*" Paul's parents "*raised him well*" by "*taking him to church*" and "*inspired him with the necessary spiritual values that we all share*" – values which "*guided him to his new position today.*" At this point the boss said, "*Paul, where are your parents?*" Looking to the audience, he then said, "*Let's all give them a round of applause for the exceptional job they have done helping Paul become the person he is today.*" At that moment, those who knew Paul well shared the same thought, "*Oh my God!*" As the applause began, Paul replied, "*Uh, actually sir, they're dead.*"

Needless to say, it was an uncomfortable moment for everyone, but the evening moved on. Next came the steak dinner in Paul's honor. It would have seemed funny if it had been planned as a joke. But it wasn't. Those who knew Paul well couldn't agree on what was more bizarre: the menu, or the fact that the meal started with an unexpected Christian blessing by the boss. Most people in the room had no idea what was really happening because the events seemed normal to them. But Paul wasn't "normal." He was both a religious agnostic and vegetarian.

We can't stress this point enough – we must be careful when making assumptions about those whom we desire to influence. Unless we only assemble teams of people who think like us (and then we have an entirely different set of problems), we have to make a concerted effort to see the world from each and every person's perspective. Otherwise, we have little hope of really understanding what motivates them and how they might respond to what we say and do.

We must remember that leadership is fundamentally about influencing others. This isn't to suggest that leaders must pander to the minority beliefs of every follower, but leaders do have a responsibility to create an inclusive environment where everyone feels comfortable. It would not have been difficult to change a few aspects of the evening we just described to create a vastly different reality for Paul. Offer a vegetarian option and a moment of silence rather than a religious blessing before dinner for all to observe in the way they see fit. Leaders should never create a situation where others are made to feel unnecessarily uncomfortable and excluded.

It is natural for human beings to make assumptions about everything all the time and look for evidence to prove themselves correct. The punch line is quite simple – not everyone thinks like you, and you should never allow yourself to assume they do. To the extent you work to find evidence which might refute your perspective, you may learn a lot about others you did not know.

Ladies and Gentlemen (p.106)

As noted by prominent business researchers Lee Bolman and Terrance Deal, organizational activities can be likened to theatrical events.[1] Yes, we are all actors in this organizational production. Those leaders (or rather, "actors") who play their parts well, wear the appropriate costumes, use the right props, read the audience and play to the crowd can be highly successful. Unfortunately, in organizational theater there is no backstage, no dressing room, and no rehearsal. Leaders are always performing even when they think that they are not.

Theater is based upon the art of acting, which not surprisingly also shares the same root word found in "enactment." When you read through other leadership books, enactment is one topic that is almost never discussed. This is a shame. Whether leaders realize it or not, they are fundamentally responsible for creating the organizational reality in which they operate whether they intend to or not. And it isn't just confined to leaders, every actor impacts the system and the resultant reality.

Everyone in an organization is an actor. Organizational actors (*e.g.*, executives, managers, administrative staff) each assume roles in an organization and then behave in a manner that they believe is consistent with the role they have assumed. The *inter-action* between players creates a social reality in the organization. Leaders can choose roles not only for themselves, but also for their followers guiding behavior in a way that achieves a desired end-state of the interaction. Intentionally taking an enactment approach can create an organizational reality that had not existed before. People act differently not by choice, but rather by their own expectations to behave in a manner consistent with "organizational theater."

The best example of enactment is probably attributable to Philip Zimbardo in his 1971 prison experiment at Stanford University.[2] Zimbardo recruited undergraduate student volunteers to play the roles of guards or prisoners. Roles were assigned by the researchers. They agreed to allow themselves to be locked in the basement of the psychology building on campus for two weeks and were paid $75 per day (in today's dollars). The "guards" were given uniforms, mirrored sunglasses and batons while the "prisoners" were given poor fitting smocks, no underwear and flip-flops. Each "prisoner" was assigned a number and thereafter never referred to by name. Zimbardo informed the "guards" during the initial briefing that:

> *"You can create in the prisoners feelings of boredom, a sense of fear to some degree. You can create a notion of arbitrariness that their life is totally controlled by us, by the system, you, me, and they'll have no privacy... We're going to take away their individuality in various ways. In general what all this leads to is a sense of powerlessness. That is, in this situation we'll have all the power and they'll have none."*

Likewise, the "prisoners" were told simply to wait in their homes to be called on the day the experiment began. Without any other warning, they were "charged" with armed robbery, arrested by the local police department and brought to "jail" at Stanford.

Within just a few days, without prompting from the research team, the "prisoners" and "guards" rapidly adapted to their roles, stepped well beyond the boundaries of what the researchers had predicted and began enacting a reality that was indistinguishable from a real prison. The guards began abusing the prisoners and the prisoners began revolting against the guards. The experiment became so real that it was terminated after only six days instead of lasting the entire two-week planned duration.

Regardless of the format, be it *Late-Night with David Letterman* or "a prison reality," leaders, the organizational reality is your show. You write the script every single day. Do you prefer a comedy or tragedy?

Exemplars (p.108)

We should take great care when crowning our organizational exemplars. It's very hard to hide who we are. Somehow the good and bad in us oozes out and is seen by everyone. The incongruities of leaders lacking character writing core value statements is almost, but not quite as obvious as a father warning his son of the dangers of smoking while lighting a cigarette.

When new employees want to know how best to fit in with an organization, they need look no further than the exemplars who represent the proper values, beliefs, and attitudes of the very best employees. To employees seeking success, these exemplars trump company policies when there is a question regarding expected organizational behavior.

Organizations need exemplars because of the critical role they serve within their cultures. Exemplars are the ideal role models for all members to emulate. Exemplars are supposed to manifest the desired knowledge, skills, attitudes and core values of the organization. Those who have ambitions of rising to higher levels in the organization often look to exemplars as a guide to navigate the ambiguity of how to behave when choices are required. The problem is that exemplars are people too. They make mistakes, say things they regret and make choices they later wish they could change.

Exemplars frequently find themselves as leaders within their organization with everyone looking to them as the "model" organizational member. After all, the organization promoted them and determined that they manifested the necessary attributes to lead others. One morning, they wake up and find out that they are the organizational exemplar. Can they live up to the expectations of perfection?

At one level, of course not. No one can live up to such high expectations. But that is precisely the point. An exemplar is not simply an artifact within an organizational culture that serves as a guide to everyone else. They actually form the ideal model for themselves to emulate. That is the irony.

Battered (p.110)

Most people report in surveys that they are moderately satisfied with their jobs. That is, until they ponder what an ideal work environment would be like and then consider how close or far their job is to being that ideal job for them. It turns out, after a bit of thought, people will often admit they aren't really as happy as they want to believe they are.

We have come to understand that the reason why so many people believe that they are satisfied with their jobs is because they don't know any better. Everything is relative and we don't all have knowledge of other great jobs as a reference point with which to compare our mediocre jobs. If you've had both arms and legs shackled to the floor for twenty years and finally have an arm released, things tend to look pretty good from your perspective.

If more leaders had a sophisticated understanding of power, perhaps we would observe less abusive behavior in organizations. Relying more on one's genuine expertise and mutual respect to influence organizational members can drastically reduce any incentives to act out in abusive ways.

If we find ourselves being cruel to control those around us, we should consider the impact we are having on the climate of our organizations. In our experience, leaders who make managing their organizational climate a top priority typically find that most other problems disappear. There is simply no room for power trips in organizations today – they are poisonous.

Creativity and Diversity (p.112)

Let's be honest. Most of us don't care about diversity as much as we care about validation. We feel validated when our ideas are shared by others and we feel threatened when they aren't. Viewpoints expressed by colleagues which differ from ours can threaten us. We normally listen to divergent ideas and opinions and then seek confirmation from the group that our ideas are correct. We have a long way to go before our organizations are true bastions of diversity. Pretending that we're already diverse and inclusive isn't helping us get there any faster.

We believe the word "diversity" is misunderstood. Think about your work environment and consider how diverse it is. What criteria do you use to assess diversity? If you are like most, you probably gravitate to the aspects that are most observable: race, gender, religion and perhaps sexual orientation.

These categories are unquestionably important, primarily because in the United States, federal laws have mandated that larger organizations provide equal opportunity to everyone. But along the way, researchers have discovered that *diversity matters* when it comes to organizational performance. Companies with greater levels of diversity routinely outperform others that are less diverse. So what's the connection between having a different skin color or an X versus a Y chromosome and organizational effectiveness? Absolutely nothing. We allow ourselves to be tricked if we are lured into believing differences in someone's genetic attributes has anything to do with his ability to contribute to the organization.

Diversity is fundamentally about ideas. Differences in skin color, gender, religious affiliation and sexual orientation tend to create very different individual life experiences. These varied experiences often translate into differences in how we perceive the world. Diversity is the immunization with which an organization can inoculate itself against groupthink and stagnation. By bringing a confluence of different perspectives together, leaders can more easily envision opportunities that were never before visible because their perspectives are broadened.

Diversity, as defined by law, is a good thing, but merely complying with the law isn't enough. Leaders must nurture diversity of thought in an organization and ensure that minority opinions or "wild ideas" are not summarily dismissed. Every individual matters in an organization and leaders have a responsibility to ensure all have a chance to fully explain and develop their ideas in an open and inclusive environment.

Using the singing metaphor from the *Creativity and Diversity* story, we see the importance of leaders ensuring every choir member has ample opportunity to solo once in a while in order to hear his or her own voice. It is necessary for each of us to voice our ideas aloud every now and then to improve our ability to harmonize with others. To the extent that diversity is embraced in a culture where ideas matter, rarely will anyone sing out of tune.

Priming (p.114)

Effective leaders understand the power of priming. You really can't create a great organizational culture without priming employees. The language and expressions leaders use on a daily basis prime followers to think in a certain way. It's one of the subconscious processes which occurs continuously in all organizations.

Have you ever been told *not to think* of something, and then immediately, you find that it is the *only thing* you can think about? For instance, *do not* think of a pink elephant. Think of anything else, but no thoughts whatsoever relating to pink elephants.

Consider the following puzzle:

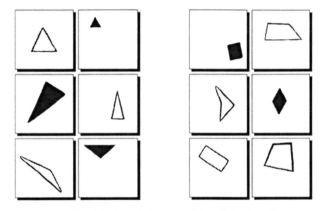

Puzzle #6 by M.M Bongard (Foundalis, 2006).

On the left are examples of things that are in the category, whereas on the right are things that are *not in the category.* The question is, "What's the category?"

Pause here for a moment and consider Puzzle #6. What do the objects on the left have in common with each other, and how does this "rule" exclude all the objects on the right? What can you discern from the left side of the puzzle to help you understand the relationship on the right side?

(Don't keep reading unless you are ready for the answer).

What concepts did you first use to try to solve the puzzle? If you are like most people, you had no idea where to begin, so you probably considered color. Some are black and some are white, but none are pink. Yes, that's right. By now, the pink elephant probably disappeared from your mind, but somehow the concept of color remained in the background. You had been primed to see color. The answer to the puzzle does not lie in the color, but rather the shape. The objects on the left all have three sides whereas all of the objects on the right all have four-sides. *Look back at the puzzle. Can you see it now?*

Let's try another one:

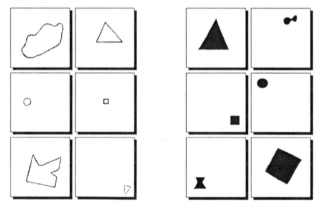

Puzzle #3 by M.M Bongard (Foundalis, 2006).

How did you do? You probably figured out Puzzle #3 pretty easily. If you didn't see it immediately, it is probably because you likely first considered the shape of the objects because that is what you were just "primed" to do by the previous puzzle. But as soon as you real-ized (even if unconsciously) that there was no shape relationship, you probably reverted back to what you knew and that was color. All the objects on the left are white and all the objects on the right are black.

If you are like most people, you may find Puzzle #19 on the next page a bit more difficult. The concepts of shape and color don't seem to help. You need to be primed with a new concept, but you aren't getting any external help. So absent any more priming, you are left to struggle with trying to figure out for yourself what concepts might be useful.

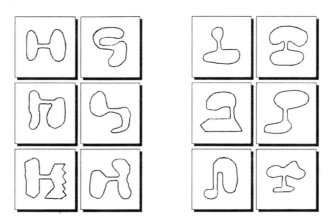

Puzzle #19 by M.M Bongard (Foundalis, 2006).

You might try "round" or "zig-zag" or "curve" or "symmetry." If at this point you haven't figured it out, you probably won't because we just primed you with all the concepts that will prevent you from being successful. Again, more pink elephants.

But now consider Puzzle #7:

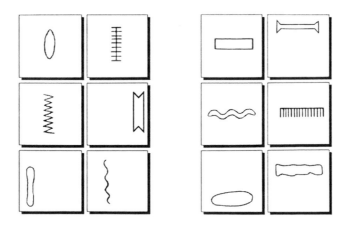

Puzzle #7 by M.M Bongard (Foundalis, 2006).

Once again, if the answer isn't obvious to you, it is likely because you have been primed *not* to notice the orientation. But as soon as you consider the rotation of the objects, you can probably differentiate between the left and right sides of the puzzle quite easily. The objects on the left side are oriented vertically whereas the objects on the right side are oriented horizontally.

Now, go back to Puzzle #19 on the previous page. Armed with the new concepts of "vertical" and "horizontal," can you solve it now? Of course you can. You have been primed.

The importance of priming emerged in the 1960s in the fields of computer science and psychology when scientists became interested in artificial intelligence. In addition to the Russian computer scientist Mikhail Bongard,[3] who designed the puzzles you just saw, Harvard psychologist Richard Herrnstein[4] was simultaneously performing priming experiments with pigeons. He would show them slides of different leaves and reward them when they pecked at oak leaves but not anything else. But this particular experiment was more than a replication of the famed Pavlov's Dog experiment. It turns out that Herrnstein was able to prime pigeons to learn things that would have previously been unimaginable for an animal with such a small brain. Over the decades that followed, researchers concluded that priming is fundamental to learning behavior.

What does this priming exercise tell us about being an effective leader? Consider the prevalence of mission and vision statements in organizations. Why do organizational leaders believe it necessary to frame and hang them everywhere? That's right, organizational members are being primed. And what about the clichés about the *"power of positive thinking"* and *"the importance of maintaining a positive attitude?"* Whether they are aware of it or not, articulating such phrases can prime followers. When you are the leader, how you act, what you say, what you wear, what car you drive – matters.

Try a little experiment on yourself. For one hour, carry a strained expression on your face. Do not be over the top, just be devoid of happiness and pleasantries. Observe how others act in your presence. Take note of how you feel and how you communicate with others.

On another day, also for one hour, carry a happy expression and go out of your way to engage in pleasantries. Again, observe how others act in your presence. Take note of how you feel and how you and others communicate. To observe priming in action is the first step to consciously controlling it and creating the optimal culture for an organization.

(Just to prevent any undue frustration in the event you didn't see the relationship in Puzzle #19, it was in the orientation of the neck of the objects.[5]*)*

The Grand Illusion (p.116)

If you have ever attended training sessions promoting diversity, you've likely heard the word "tolerance" quite a bit. While promoting *tolerance* might seem like a reasonable approach to embracing diversity, we disagree.

Take the word *tolerate*. Despite its meaning "to put up with" or "to endure," it has become a generally-accepted approach to dealing with others who are different in some way. So what does it mean to be tolerant? Well, first, you must note a difference in someone else such as eye color, gender, weight, accent, etc. Second, you must choose *not* to allow the difference to impact your relationship with that person. All that really separates tolerant behavior from intolerant behavior is a conscious effort to suppress a desire within ourselves to shun others who are different than we are. Thus, the mere use of the word *tolerance* can lead us to believe that we don't have to like the difference observed in another, but we have to put up with it.

When leaders preach "tolerance" as the guiding approach to human relations, one of the messages often heard by others is that they have to put up with co-workers who are different whether they like it or not. When you think about tolerance in these terms, there doesn't seem to be much of a difference between tolerance and intolerance.

This doesn't mean that diversity training is bad. In fact, diversity training exists out of necessity. Organizations must establish a baseline for people from different backgrounds to come together and work with one another in the pursuit of institutional goals. Without such training, individual attitudes and beliefs towards others might otherwise go unchecked, leading to bigotry and harassment. Therefore, it is necessary for diversity training to illustrate the harmful effects of stereotypes. But in doing so, such programs often fall short by failing to consider the secondary effects which discussions about stereotypes so often invoke. By preaching the need not to discriminate on the basis of race, religion, sexual orientation, political affiliation or gender, we may inadvertently categorize people without even meaning to do so, particularly in organizations with lower degrees of diversity in highlighted categories (e.g. mostly male, mostly white, mostly Christian, mostly Republican, etc.)

Since the desired outcome of any diversity training program should be to foster a sense of awareness on the part of the trainee, training directors should consider to what extent the training might create a sense of *in-groups* and *out-groups* by focusing attention on any particular highlighted attribute. Psychological research has repeatedly demonstrated that in-groups tend to develop a sense of superiority towards out-groups, even under the most artificially created laboratory experimental conditions (*e.g.* the Stanford prison study discussed earlier). Out-groups can be tolerated, but they are often tolerated as an inferior group and the very act of toleration reinforces the sense of superiority the in-group holds. Such a secondary effect could be quite harmful and counterproductive to the original intent of programs designed to teach "tolerance."

We believe diversity training should instead focus on the individual level. We all know that no two people are the same. Yet, when we encounter someone who appears to be very similar to ourselves, we can't help but immediately assume they think like we do, hold our same values and likely agree with our perspectives. Similarly, when we encounter someone who is different, we become cautious and judgmental. Like it or not, it's natural for us to act this way as human beings unless we deliberately train ourselves to become aware of how useless superficial judgments are.

Diversity training programs teach us not to discriminate on irrelevant attributes because research has repeatedly shown that such variables simply don't correlate with job performance. Rarely is much attention given to the need to tolerate green-eyed people, but a great deal of tolerance training continues to focus on attributes such as race, gender, religion or sexual orientation promoting a generic message that *"discrimination is bad."* Hearing this, we are often led to believe that we should avoid making discriminating judgments at all. But perhaps this is where the wrong message is being communicated. As Harvard researcher Ellen Langer notes, the act of discrimination is not only *good* – it is *absolutely necessary.*[6] We agree.

Think about it. In its purest form, discrimination is an essential element in the daily functioning of both organizations and individuals. Organizations routinely discriminate between people to identify the best-fit candidates for a particular job. Society wouldn't tolerate blind pilots, asthmatic firefighters or autistic neurosurgeons. Under United States law, it is entirely permissible for organizations to discriminate between competing candidates to select whom they believe to be the "best-qualified," provided legitimate criteria exist by which the discrimination can be made. At the individual level, all of us demonstrate discriminating behavior on a daily basis. Without active and healthy discrimination, we would have a hard time getting through the day.

We make discriminating choices all the time. In doing so, we often find ourselves taking unconscious shortcuts to arrive at preliminary judgments using the attributes and characteristics we can readily observe and define. When such cognitive shortcuts are used, the resulting value from our judgments is often minimal to nonexistent. Problems begin to emerge when we allow ourselves to believe that identifying differences among irrelevant attributes are meaningful. When we find ourselves making judgments based on seeing someone in strange clothes or hearing them speak in a foreign language, we must be mindful that our conclusions are probably unwarranted. According to Langer, to be of any value, we mustn't stop our discrimination at these high levels, but continue to take our discriminating judgments to the extreme and look at all attributes that may be relevant in evaluating someone's worthiness.

When we really stop to make thoughtful, relevant comparisons by *discriminating as much as we can,* it becomes immediately clear that no two human beings are the same. Once this level of discrimination is achieved, our judgments based on someone's ability to do a job become far more accurate and relevant. When leaders make a habit of fully discriminating across the range of relevant performance and capability attributes, active efforts to promote *in-group* and *out-group* events such as "Diversity Month" become immediately obsolete because *every day* should be a celebration of diversity in an effective organization.

Creating a sense of tolerance for individual differences among organization members is often a necessary first step along a continuum to foster an inclusive and cohesive environment. If the ultimate goal is to develop a sense of perceived equity between individuals in an organization that transcends individual differences, then perhaps if leaders taught members to *discriminate more,* organizations would have a greatly reduced need for *tolerance* training.

A JOURNEY INTO CONTROL

Monitoring

Integrity

Teamwork

Lunchrooms

Where You Should Be

Trust

"As we look ahead into the next century, leaders will be those who empower others."
—*Bill Gates*

"Habit can be the best of servants or the worst of masters."
—*Nathaniel Emmons*

"We have created trouble for ourselves in organizations by confusing control with order...

* * *

Without reflection, we go blindly on our way, creating more unintended consequences, and failing to achieve anything useful."
—*Margaret J. Wheatley*

MONITORING

"10:07:54 a.m. Eastern Time" read the clock across the top of the computer screen.

"I thought computers were supposed to make our lives better," mumbled Kiesha under her breath. She had to go to the bathroom pretty badly, but she knew that she could probably hold it in for another twenty minutes. By that time, she would have answered at least another three calls and she would be on target to meet her morning goal.

Just below the time display on her computer screen, the "average utilization" metric was listed and colored green. She was above 97%. So far, so good. That is why she couldn't leave right now, because if she did, those four minutes to the bathroom and back would count against her.

Across from Kiesha sat Michael. Michael hated this new management information system that the company introduced several months ago and he was outspoken about it. He filed a grievance with the union claiming "cruel and unusual punishment." Human beings cannot work like this, being watched every second, literally, of the work day. He saw himself as a good employee. He was routinely complimented by those who called him for being so pleasant and helpful. In fact, he received the company's Customer Satisfaction Award last year. Not bad out of 300 call-center employees.

The problem was that Michael wasn't nearly as productive as everyone thought. He spent far too much time talking with customers compared to his fellow employees. On average, he only fielded 71.42% as many calls as the most productive call-center employee, and his average utilization metric was always yellow – 91%. Michael liked to keep a log of whom he spoke with. He also kept track of information that helped him remember "the more challenging" callers as he quickly learned that they would likely call again and ask for him. He prided himself on being able to surprise repeat-callers by remembering who they were. Getting the annual customer service award was a piece of cake for Michael. He got it three years in a row. He had the whole system figured out.

And then they changed it. Suddenly he became a marginal employee. His supervisor called him in just yesterday to counsel him on his continued marginal performance. He couldn't take it anymore. He quit right there on the spot.

The person who replaced Michael was Dana. She was now the face that Kiesha saw when she looked up from her cubicle, not Michael's. She missed Michael.

Yikes! The average utilization metric just went yellow – 92%. On no, she shouldn't have been daydreaming. Now she would have to wait until lunch to go to the bathroom. She didn't have a choice. She needed this job.

Reflections:

° Are you controlled at work? If so, how?

° Do you like when others control what you do?

° Do you like to control what others do?

° Assuming leaders have a responsibility to control those under them, how should they do it?

(Authors' Reflections on page 155)

INTEGRITY

Consider two stories about integrity.

The first perspective:

After an entire semester in an ethics class, a frustrated young woman approached her professor and confessed, *"Professor, after spending hours reading and sitting through class, I am still not sure I know how to define 'integrity.' At one level, it seems so simple, but yet after taking this class, I feel like it is something much more. So I have to ask, what is integrity?"*

The professor smiled and replied, *"You seem to understand the concept quite well. But if you are looking for a definition, that part is easy. To the extent you have integrity, you are who you appear to be."*

Second perspective:

At a Berkshire-Hathaway Annual Shareholders Meeting, a young man stepped up to the microphone and asked Warren Buffett what characteristics he looked for when he hired people. Without hesitation, Mr. Buffett replied, *"Well, it's quite simple. I look for three things: intelligence, energy and integrity."*

He then went on to explain that of the three, integrity was the most important, because without it, the *"first two will kill you."*

Reflections:

° How would you define integrity?

° What did Warren Buffett seem to know about the challenges a leader faces?

° Describe the relationship between integrity and character. Are they the same thing?

° What are essential values for a "person of character"?

° Do you see a relationship between integrity and control?

(Authors' Reflections on page 157)

TEAMWORK

As they walked out of the conference room, Jan looked at Myra and rolled her eyes. She didn't intend for Brian to see her and it didn't matter that he did. He apparently shared the same thought, as was every other person walking out of the weekly meeting. *Dan just didn't get it.* Ever since he joined the group, teamwork had eroded. No matter what the issue was, Dan always seemed to have a different perspective. When the monthly reports came in showing profitability increasing beyond expectations, instead of agreeing with everyone that the team's performance was the reason for the increase, Dan would question to what extent recent accounting changes or decreases in supplier costs might have impacted the figures. No matter what emerged, you could rest assured that if everyone else was troubled by it, Dan wouldn't be. He never seemed to agree with anyone regardless of the topic. Up until he arrived, everyone seemed to agree on just about everything. Things used to work so much better.

The bigger problem wasn't so much that Dan was so disagreeable; it was that he did it so well. His calm demeanor and even-tempered approach made it very difficult for anyone else to challenge him. He always remained focused on the issue and kept saying, "but when we refer to the data..." It was terribly frustrating because meetings that should have taken ten minutes seemed to drag on for an hour or more, week after week.

If anyone was to blame, it was probably Dennis. Dennis was their team leader and he was the one who hired Dan onto the team shortly after he took over. What had become clear was that Dennis obviously had no backbone. Any *real* team leader would have recognized long ago that Dan hindered the efficiency and teamwork that existed before Dennis took over.

The entire team was anxious when Dennis was appointed. Any change in leadership always makes people nervous. But after a few weeks, everyone could see that Dennis would be great to work with because he always seemed to go along with the consensus of the group. He fostered a culture of teamwork.

As they walked down the hall together, Jan turned to Myra and said, *"The worst part about it is that Dan is so patient. He often gets us to agree with him by wearing us down. Even today, I finally agreed with Dan just to end the misery of a longer meeting. Funny though, I can't remember if I was agreeing with him or he was agreeing with me. Arghh! See, that's what I mean! He's so good at frustrating everyone, we don't even know which ideas are ours anymore!"*

Myra replied, *"It's too bad profits increased 60% since Dennis and Dan joined the team. Dennis may never understand how much better off we would be if he would focus on improving our teamwork."*

Reflections:

° How much teamwork do you want in your organization?

° Which loyalty is more important: loyalty to your peers or loyalty to the organization?

° How can you know if you have the right people on your team?

(Authors' Reflections on page 160)

LUNCHROOMS

The lunchroom wasn't very large. It had four round tables, two microwaves, a refrigerator and a sink. At noon it was always full, almost uncomfortably so, as six or seven people often squeezed around tables that were meant for five. The room was noisy and filled with chatter as each person competed to be heard by the others. Given the layout of the rest of the building, the lunchroom was an odd scene.

There was really no need to cram twenty-five people into the small lunchroom. Unlike what is found in most offices today, every employee had a private office. Most offices had small refrigerators in a corner and many had coffee-makers as well. A few even had microwave ovens. It was almost completely unnecessary for employees to venture out of their well-proportioned and uniquely decorated habitats. Yet they all did.

Although the boss told no one, she kept close watch on the lunchroom. She was never conspicuous, but she made it a habit to rinse out her coffee mug at various times on various days during the lunch period.

(The following endings describe two nearly identical stories that take place in very different organizations.)

The first ending:

As the boss walked into the lunchroom, no one noticed her. They were too busy talking about, well, anything. She would smile. A few people would inevitably see her and smile back, then continue their eager discussions about how they would change the world. The boss of this highly effective organization knew that the organizational climate was the only thing that ever needed to be managed. Nothing else mattered.

The second ending:

As the boss walked into the lunchroom, the room fell silent. She was very angry that the door was closed again. She kept propping it open, but when she would leave the employees would invariably close it. The boss of this highly dysfunctional organization knew that she had to retain control over her employees. Nothing else mattered.

Reflections:

- ° What was it that drew employees into these particular lunchrooms?

- ° How important is it for a boss to keep close tabs on a lunchroom?

- ° How would you characterize the relationship between the amount of talking in the hallway and organizational climate?

- ° Do you see a connection between organizational climate and productivity?

(Authors' Reflections on page 161)

WHERE YOU SHOULD BE

All the new hires arrived for orientation on time. The managing director stood by the door and gave an individual welcome to each person as they walked in. When everyone was seated, the director gave an additional welcome to the group then discussed the organization's vision, mission and goals for the coming year. She mentioned how each person, by name, fit into the vision, mission and goals of the company. Next, she spent some time talking about the importance of the organization's culture. Lastly, she briefly highlighted a few policies. When she was done, she opened up the floor for questions. A man sitting in the back asked her what the organization's policy was regarding taking time off for events such as attending his kid's soccer games and music recitals.

The director responded, *"We don't really have a policy on where you should be."*

The man looked disappointed.

The director smiled and continued, *"As far as we are concerned, wherever you are, that is where you should be."*

Reflections:

° Could an organization operate effectively with such a policy?

° What would happen if the above statement became policy in your organization?

° How would you feel if your boss asked you where you were every time you missed a moment at work?

(Authors' Reflections on page 162)

TRUST

You just can't trust people anymore. People seem to start out honest enough, showing up to work on time, staying a full day, sometimes even a little longer, trying their best, wanting to do a good job-an honest day's work for an honest day's pay. Then, inexplicably, they start to take advantage of the system. First, it's coming in a little late. Next, it's leaving early. Then, they start taking sick days when they're not really sick. Allergies don't count. We all have allergies.

Calling people out on their lack of responsibility doesn't help, either. They just get sneakier. And their excuses get a bit more creative. Cracking down with stronger attendance policies doesn't work. They just lead to better excuses. People will figure out what excuses will protect them legally and will use them. Maybe it's all the preservatives in food these days. You just can't trust people anymore. *But what if you did?*

Reflections:

   ° Do you trust your boss?

   ° Can your boss trust you? (*Really?*)

   ° To what extent does trusting behavior towards others impact their behavior?

   ° How does it feel not to be trusted?

   ° What changes when you feel as though you are trusted at work?

   ° How do you build an environment of trust in an organization?

   ° Would you really want to?

(Authors' Reflections on page 163)

WHAT IS THE KEY TO CONTROL?

Perhaps the single most important concept in organizations (and in life) is that of control. And yet, so many leaders take control for granted, almost as a given. After all, that's what rules are for, right? Without control, actions would be random and unpredictable. Some might even say 'chaotic.'

A number of years ago, Michael Barnsley[1] (a mathematician and entrepreneur) appeared on public television and introduced us to *The Chaos Game.* It went like this:

> (1) Take out a sheet of paper and draw three end points of an equilateral triangle. Label each of the points A, B and C as follows:

A
°

B °   ° C

(2) Now choose any random point within the triangle and draw a dot.

(3) Roll a die.

> a. If it comes up 1 or 2, *measure half the distance* from your current point and point A, and plot a new point here (draw another dot.)
>
> b. If it comes up 3 or 4, *measure half the distance* from your current point and point B, and plot a new point here (draw another dot.)
>
> c. If it comes up 5 or 6, *measure half the distance* from your current point and point C, and plot a new point here (draw another dot.)

(4) Continue to repeat Step 3 using the new point as the next starting point. Do this for about a million iterations and something pretty amazing emerges.

Can you guess what it is? Consider for a moment, what would you expect to emerge from repeating this very simple (and rather boring) exercise?

From what most anyone would expect to be a mess of dots, a highly regular pattern (known as a *Sierpiński Triangle*) emerges. This pattern of self-similarity is known in mathematics as a *fractal*. No matter what part of the image you analyze, you discover the same pattern infinitely repeated. The larger image is comprised of smaller images of itself. Fractals are just one aspect of a field of mathematics know as *Chaos Theory*.

However, Chaos Theory is more than math equations. Many people find fractals fascinating because they illustrate how order can emerge from apparent randomness. There are many classes of fractals, but there is one other type of fractal that is of particular interest. The specific type of fractal discovered by meteorologist

A

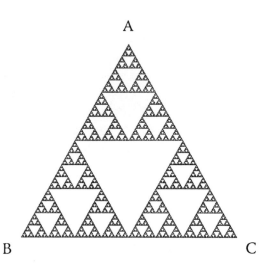

B   C

Fractal produced by "The Chaos Game:" A Sierpiński Triangle [2]

Edward Lorenz gave rise to what has commonly become known as "the butterfly effect."[3]

Lorenz reasoned small atmospheric disturbances caused by a butterfly flapping its wings in China could lead to far larger disturbances in Texas (*e.g.,* tornadoes, hurricanes, *etc.*). Surely, the butterfly can't be accused of *causing* a tornado, but because of the interaction and interdependencies of complex systems, Lorenz demonstrated how the eventual outcomes (or equilibrium states) are highly sensitive to the initial conditions of a system. Lorenz demonstrated how some fractals can be highly ordered and yet completely unpredictable. At a micro-level, the observer can never know how the individual elements in the system will behave, but at a macro-level, the behavior of the system is highly regular and predictable as if it were bound by an invisible force. This phenomenon, which seemingly establishes boundaries for elements within a system, came to be known as a "strange attractor."

But what does this all have to do with control?

Authors James Gleick[4] and Meg Wheatley[5] were two of the first authors to relate the concepts of chaos theory to practical issues outside the domain of mathematics. In her book, *Leadership and the New Science*, Wheatley frames organizations as chaotic systems. Because organizations are made up of people, each pursuing their own individual purposes while simultaneously working with one another towards a shared organizational purpose, it is nearly impossible for leaders to predict individual behavior of any one person if viewing the organizations through the traditional "leadership lens." But if one were to "zoom out" and take a more macro view of an organization, the otherwise seemingly chaotic behavior at the individual level translates into something far more regular at a higher level. Like the strange attractors which seem to bound Lorenz's fractal, so too are there similar strange attractors in organizations which seem to bound individual behavior.

In comparing highly effective organizations with those appearing to be less effective, Wheatley observed the power a leader's values and vision had on employee behavior. It wasn't even the vision or values that acted as the strange attractor, but rather, it was meaning and sense of purpose which had emerged within each employee. She also noted the most effective organizations had a fractal nature, meaning there was an observable level of self-similarity no matter where you looked (like Barnsley's *Sierpiński Triangle*). The values espoused by senior management were the same values articulated by not only junior executives, but also the shop floor worker, the custodian and the receptionist. Yes, it was seemingly that simple. Like the fractal pictures, no matter what part you observe, you see the same pattern – a *shared vision*.

Effective organizations depend upon leaders to communicate the core values in such a way that no matter where you look, everyone knows what these values are and what they mean. In exceptional organizations, employees derive meaning and purpose from the core values expressed in the performance of their day-to-day job. It is one thing to say you have an organizational core value of "*Integrity First*," but unless every employee values integrity personally, they are just buzz words. Great leaders create meaning for their employees within the organization and this meaning connects everyone with a shared sense of purpose.

Are you still wondering what this has to do with control? If so, consider this – if you have a system characterized by order without predictability, is the system in control?

Reflecting back to Barnsley's Chaos Game, we never know where the next point will be; after all, it's random. But it can't be just anywhere. No, it must be "within" bounds. If we construct very simple rules to bound the system, behavior within the system tends to be random, but predictably so. This may be one of the most important lessons for any leader to digest. Simple rules could lead to drastic results, good or bad. Complex systems are highly sensitive to initial conditions. To the extent organizations are bounded by the proper leadership philosophy as a strange attractor, perhaps it isn't necessary for leaders to attempt to control every part of their organization. At the micro-level, behavior might seem random, but at the macro-level, leaders should be able to predict the general patterns of behavior within the organization as well as the patterns of those comprising it.

When we look at some of the most effective organizations we encountered, the following tenets tend to emerge:

(1) The organization creates value.

(2) Leaders are highly competent and well-versed in management with a clear vision of the organization's purpose.

(3) The organization's culture is built upon a foundation of inclusion, respect and trust.

As a leader, you must decide how to maintain control over those you serve. The choice is quite simple: you can force compliance or you can create an environment in which those who work for you *want* to comply. If you choose the latter, *you are going to have to trust people*. You'll have to create a strange attractor – that sense of purpose – and then let everyone do as they will. You might be surprised. Although you may never know who is going to be in at 8:00 a.m. or how long a lunch hour might last, don't be surprised if your outputs increase like never before.

But did we mention you *really* have to trust your people? You can't pretend. They'll know. And if you are genuinely sincere, you might find yourself in control of the organization in ways you never imagined. Sure, it might look chaotic, but isn't that the point?

As far as we are concerned, everything a leader needs to understand about *control* is captured in the illustration on the following page.

This drawing was conceived as a variant of one of our favorite creative works by Douglas Hofstadter entitled *"Mu"* from the *"Ant Fugue"* in his Pulitzer Prize winning book *Gödel, Escher Bach.*[6]

AUTHORS' REFLECTIONS...*On Control*

Monitoring (p.138)

How does a father keep his teenage daughter from getting into the back seats of boys' cars? If you have children, this is a thought that either has crossed or will cross your mind someday. The fundamental question is, "To what extent can you control your child's behavior if you aren't there?" The answer? Thanks to the marvels of modern technology, you'd like to believe you can control it 100% of the time. But can you, really? Surely you can enable her cell phone with a GPS tracking device to send real-time location updates to your home computer. But then, what if she doesn't keep her phone with her at all times? That's where the camera comes in. Yes, you can install wireless cameras inside the car to watch her every move. But what if they park and get out of the car? Or what if they take his car? Well, then, perhaps you are left with old technology – the private investigator who has been following them all night. There is no doubt, *you are certainly in control*. But what if she finds out that you are watching her every move? We like to believe we are in control of those who depend on us, but are we? Are we really in control, or are we just fooling ourselves with an *illusion of control*? Can we control others who don't want to be controlled?

Effective leaders recognize both the necessity for controlling behavior as well as the limits of their influence. Control is one of the crucial functions of management, if not the most important. How to control others without creating a hostile or adversarial situation, however, is anything but trivial.

There are two basic philosophies to which a leader can subscribe. One perspective is based upon the notion of obtrusive (hands-on) control while the other is rooted in unobtrusive (inconspicuous) control. Whereas the obtrusive approach is most concerned with inputs, the unobtrusive approach is more concerned with outputs.

The leader who opts for a hands-on, input-driven style of control tends to subscribe to the "*do time*" philosophy. This is the boss that monitors when you arrive, when you take your breaks and when you leave. He ensures that your lunch hour isn't a minute longer than it should be and that you give the organization "a fair day's work for a fair day's wage." If you haven't worked for a boss like this, consider how it might make you feel day after day. If you have experienced this type of work environment, then your heart is likely beating a bit faster than it was a moment ago. In either case, ask yourself how much extra effort you would want to put forth everyday for a boss like this? Especially at 4:50 p.m. – how much effort would you exert for the last ten minutes (or 600 seconds) of your day? 100%?

The second management philosophy is the "*do things*" approach. Instead of an input-driven perspective – how much effort or time you put forth – the focus is exclusively on output. At the end of the day (week, month, etc.), the leader evaluates the effectiveness of the employee in terms of outputs – things done directly relating to and in support of the mission of the organization.

This latter unobtrusive approach has its risks, and the most obvious is that employees will take advantage of their boss's goodwill and shirk their organizational responsibilities. The boss who opts for unobtrusive control, however, doesn't worry about his employees sitting at their desks surfing the net, or not coming in to work first thing in the morning in lieu of running personal errands. In fact, he encourages people to run the errand if doing so is necessary at that particular moment. If questioned about this, his reply should always be: "*I don't have any way to know how important that particular errand was to him. Only he was in a position to make the judgment call, and I trust him.*" This type of leader isn't so delusional to think he has any control over his employees unless they give it to him. He can't watch over everybody all day because he doesn't have time. But even if he did, he still wouldn't monitor everyone because it would only create a distrustful environment– and an illusion of control.

Yes, distrust is poison for this type of leader. More than anything else, the leader who takes the unobtrusive approach to control understands that if he can foster a trusting relationship with his employees, in the end, they will put the required effort in (and if the trust is genuine, probably far more effort than would be expected) to produce for that leader because they wouldn't want to let him down.

Most parents understand that the only way to control their children when they aren't around is to establish clear behavioral expectations and values regarding what is appropriate and what is not. They hope the child will behave as the parent desires because the child deems such behavior to be appropriate for herself. The parent trusts the child, the child knows this, and the worst thing for the child would be to disappoint her parents and *lose their trust*. Trust is the foundation of control, unless of course, you mount cameras everywhere.

Consider the following: *If you don't trust those that work for you, they can't be trusted. If you do trust them, then they can.* It might be just that simple.

Integrity (p.140)

How honest are you – really? If you are like most people, you probably like to think you subscribe to the highest level of integrity. However, there is no escaping the truth, and do you know what it is? Yes indeed, we are all human and subject to the same flaws we see in others. But when it comes to one's character, making mistakes can have far greater repercussions than putting too much milk in the pancake batter. When it comes to our reputation, we cannot simply add more flour to "right a wrong."

Have you ever done something at work that you aren't very proud of? Consider what that might be. Now ask yourself, "*Why did you do it? Did you ever try to make it right?*"

This is a common line of inquiry that we routinely take clients through during seminars on ethics. When we first tried it with a class of undergraduate students, we had no idea what we were on to. Over the years, however, we came to realize that everybody – yes, *everybody* (at least those that were being genuine) – could quickly come up with something that they had done that was of questionable integrity. But it wasn't so much *what* they did as *why* they did it. A routine confession from people with whom we had this discussion concerns the pilfering of office supplies. You know, that innocuous act of taking home pens, computer paper, and if you can believe it, even a chair! What surprised us most is not what various individuals did, but the rationalization each of them had made to themselves to justify their actions. They wanted to continue to believe that they were good and trustworthy and had to start lying to themselves to make it "all okay." More often than not, the rationalizations relied on the justification: "I earned it."

When we discuss this situation with groups, invariably someone speaks up who was appalled by such actions. We press them to see if we can get them to admit to even the most minor offense. Although it is somewhat uncommon to find a person like this, when we discover one, we typically find many others in the same organization. It seems that honest people tend to travel in herds. Or perhaps, it's something else.

In talking with groups of devoutly honest people, they tend to tell the same story. They "*would never dream of stealing paper or pencils*" because more than anything else, it was simply wrong. We believe that the fundamental difference between those who are likely to steal from their organization and those that are not comes down to how they perceive their leaders. Invariably, those individuals who observe the highest standards of honest behavior nearly always point to their boss as the reason why they wouldn't steal. They know it's wrong, their boss knows its wrong, the boss has clear standards for the highest levels of ethical behavior and anything else isn't tolerated.

Here's a test to see how you rate. Be honest with yourself: after all, no one has any idea how you are answering right now. If the result is not one with which you are satisfied, then perhaps this is the moment in your life where you make a commitment to *think differently* from this point forward.

Imagine that you and a friend walk into a convenience store on your lunch break and get a slushy drink. The drink with tax comes to $0.99. When you pay, you get a penny back. However, as you are getting into your car, you notice you were mistaken. The coin wasn't a penny, but rather a dime. Do you turn around and correct the error? What if the difference was $1.00? Would that make a difference? Or perhaps a $100 error?

Let's continue the thought experiment. Now assume that as you get into the car, you got correct change, but your friend mentions that he got a dime back rather than a penny? You tell him you are happy to wait if he wants to run in and resolve the mistake. He looks at you as if you are from Mars and says, *"Dude, its nine cents – are you kidding?"* You insist that he goes back in to correct the problem, but he refuses. Do you call the police and report him for theft? Suppose the mistake was $1.00, or $100, or even $10,000. Can you put a price on the value of honest behavior?

As it turns out, you can. Our experience indicates very few people would worry much about anything under $10 for themselves, but some readily admit they may feel a bit guilty for not going back and "making things right." However, at the same time, there are others who openly acknowledge to us that they would never turn their friend in for *any* amount. Even when pressed, they'd tell us even if their friend committed armed robbery and dashed out of the store with $10,000, they still wouldn't turn him in to authorities because *"he is my best friend and friends stick together!"* Wow.

So ask yourself:

° Are you really who you appear to be?

° Do people know the "real" you?

° Can you really be trusted?

° Do you have the capacity to trust others?

Teamwork (p.142)

Many years ago, we once worked for a person who seemingly detested meetings. It appeared he saw little value in them, or so we thought. Meeting after meeting, he would sit there and say nothing. We knew that he was the brightest and most capable person in the room (probably in the entire organization, for that matter), and yet, he'd sit there looking amused and say nothing. Sometimes we'd approach him afterwards and ask him why he never engaged. He'd smile at us with a fatherly smile and say, "*Why, you said it all; there was nothing else to say.*" We'd look at each other perplexed since as far as we could tell, the meeting was a complete waste of time. When we told him that we really didn't say anything, he would again smile and say, "*Yep.*" He was such a frustrating person to talk to at times. It seemed as if we were always the object of his Jedi mind games. This was surely why he was smiling.

Years later, after he had moved up considerably in the organization, we thought we had finally seen the end of useless meetings. Boy, were we wrong. Nothing changed. We still had the same meetings. The same people who "said nothing" still did all of the talking and the rest of us just sat there and watched the time go by.

Even after his promotion, it still took us another year to figure out why he continued to hold the same, routine meetings. Eventually, it became quite clear. When we finally believed we had correctly solved this "meeting riddle," we approached him with our answer. He simply smiled as he always did and said, "*Yep.*"

Indeed, he still frustrated us as much as he ever had in forcing us to derive the meaning of our own perceptions, but the journey he guided us on yielded much. In this particular case, he never expected to accomplish anything in a meeting. That much we had correct from the beginning. What wasn't so obvious was that what he really sought from the routine meeting was an eventual outcome of creating an effective team. As bizarre as it seemed when we first hypothesized this, it turned out to be correct.

Our leader recognized that there were different factions in the organization who would prefer not to engage with each other if left to their own choosing, so he structured our interactions in such a way that we had to engage one another routinely. That was really the only purpose that the meeting served. It forced us to sit there and engage with everyone else. Sure, there were always those few (in each faction) who had something to say that amounted to nothing more than noise, but this meeting gave them a chance to vent. As for everyone else, whether they liked it or not, they had to sit there and try to make sense out of things they heard.

The boss understood that the smaller organizational issues were ours to solve, but the largest issue was his. We were all on his team and our failure to work with each other would mean his failure as a boss. None of us ever really wanted to go to the routine meetings, but when we walked away, we always seemed to be on the same page, even if it wasn't where we had planned on being.

That's teamwork.

Lunchrooms (p.144)

It doesn't take long to determine the climate of an organization. One of the best indicators of an organization's climate can be found in its lunchroom. The lunchroom is where employees usually let their guards down a bit and forget for a moment they're at work. If leaders can create the right climate, so many other problems which are common to most organizations tend never to emerge. *Why?* With the right climate, employees internalize organizational values, feel and accept ownership and responsibility for organizational activities, and see their work with the company as part of their identity rather than just a job.

What is the conversation like around your office lunch table? If you don't have a lunch table in the office, what does that say about your organization? Anything?

Where You Should Be (p.146)

When we first heard a leader say to new employees she trusts everyone and *"wherever they are is exactly where they need to be,"* it sounded like a trick. But after reflecting on these words and recognizing that she actually meant what she said, we realized the immense power she had over us. At 8:30 a.m., sometimes people need to take their children to school and that's quite difficult if work hours are 8:00 a.m. to 5:00 p.m. So workers are faced with a real dilemma – set up morning daycare for 45-minutes each day or quit their job and find another place to work.

We remember a story based on a book by author James Autry[7] of a young lieutenant in the military who had been deployed overseas shortly after he and his wife had been reassigned to a new location where they had never before lived. She was pregnant when he deployed, and they both hoped that he would be back in time for the birth of their first child. Such is the life of a soldier. Sacrifices are regrettably part of the job, and everyone knows it – especially the soldier and his family.

Shortly after arriving at the deployed location, the soldier got word that his wife had become ill and the baby would have to be delivered prematurely. Upon hearing this, the young soldier approached his commander and asked if he could return home to be with his wife. He knew leaving early was against policy, but if the commander would grant him a waiver, he would be willing to return after the baby was born and start the deployment all over, even stay longer. He'd do anything to get a waiver to return home. The commander looked squarely at the young officer and replied, *"Son, you need to understand something. In my unit, no one gets special treatment. Your request is denied."*

Although the lieutenant was not permitted to return home, his wife gave birth, recovered from her illness and both mom and new baby girl ended up being just fine.

Decades later, the young lieutenant had transitioned to civilian life and become a successful executive in business. He never forgot about this profound experience early in his career and the importance of special treatment. Thus, he made it point to meet with every person hired into his organization. Each month, he would gather all of the newcomers and state in no uncertain terms, *"Welcome to the organization. I am the leader, and in my organization, everyone gets special treatment."*

Exceptional leaders understand that only an individual can be the real judge of where he needs to be at any moment in time. Maybe it's at work, and maybe its not. But to the extent that a boss trusts his employees and the employees trust the boss, what's the risk? The person who is trusted to come in "late" everyday will likely never need to be asked to work late or put in extra effort because they will likely feel the need to "repay" the generosity. Reciprocity, if you will. It's a bit unfair to reveal this secret of management because it does allow for those in power to exploit their employees. That's right. Trust them and they will feel indebted to you to the extent they will probably work harder than they ever have. Weird. *Want to speed up the train?* Let go.

Trust (p.147)

Trust. *It's critical.* Trust is the *foundation of control.*[8] Look *very* closely at the picture on page 154. Perhaps you didn't recognize it earlier...

A JOURNEY INTO UNDERSTANDING

"For me, it is far better to grasp the universe as it really is than to persist in delusion, however satisfying and reassuring."
—Carl Sagan

"Change before you have to."
—Jack Welch

"Yet we act as if simple cause and effect is at work. We push to find the one simple reason things have gone wrong. We look for the one action, or the one person, that created this mess. As soon as we find someone to blame, we act as if we've solved the problem. I believe that our very survival depends upon us becoming better systems thinkers."
—Margaret J. Wheatley

RELATIONSHIPS

At an off-site meeting, the consultant asked *"What is the relationship between organizations and people?"*

One manager responded, *"Organizations serve people. Organizations provide jobs, security, and health-care as well as products and services for our communities."*

Another manager said, *"People serve organizations. We try to find and work in an organization with a mission and purpose that we believe in and will have an impact on the world. Organizations take us beyond ourselves and into something bigger and greater than anything we could accomplish individually. It is an honor to serve the right organization."*

A third person spoke up, *"I think you are both correct at one level, but still missing the point of the question. By looking for a relationship between organizations and people, we allow ourselves to adopt an overly simplistic perspective. Organizations emerge from human relationships. By being in an organization, we nurture each other, develop each other, and relate with each other. Fundamentally, organizations connect us in deeply human ways. Organizations are people."*

Reflections:

° How do you see the relationship between organizations and people?

° Which perspective do you think the majority of people in your organization hold?

° How could each of these perspectives affect behavior?

° What can you do to help people in your organization expand their understanding of the relationship between themselves and their organization?

(Authors' Reflections on page 184)

FEEDBACK

It was rare to see the CEO of a multinational firm walking across the shop floor. As the arc welders cracked and cutting torches roared, the chief executive in his Armani suit strolled across the factory with his assistant in tow. No one knew quite what to make of it. There was no doubt that every worker knew they were there, but not a single person lifted his head. Each machinist kept working as diligently as he had been before the disruption.

The VIPs slowed to watch a senior machinist working a machine that they couldn't identify and manufacture a part that they couldn't describe. When the elder machinist noticed the visitors, he set his tools aside, removed his safety glasses and smiled. *"Can I help you?"* he asked. The CEO replied, *"How are things going?"*

With a serious look on his face, the machinist took off his gloves, looked directly into the CEO's eyes and asked, *"Sir, do you really want to know?"*

The CEO, with an expressionless look on his face returned the stare, then looked at his assistant and said, *"I guess not,"* and walked away.

Reflections:

  ° Do you want feedback? Really?

  ° What does it mean when people (especially superiors) say they want feedback?

  ° If the only feedback you want is praise, will you ever get the feedback you need?

  ° How do you get *real* feedback?

  ° How much feedback should you offer to others?

(Authors' Reflections on page 185)

THE CAUSE

Do you have anyone in your organization who is notorious for creating problems for everyone else?

Take Kevin. Kevin had a talent for breaking the copier at the *worst* possible times. It happened like clockwork. During moments when it seemed as if everyone needed to use the copier, undoubtedly you would find Kevin at the copier. He never made more than a few copies, but he was bad luck. The jinx. As soon as he hit the "print" button, the copier would sputter and stall. Lights would flash, an alarm would begin to beep and a low groan would ripple across the office. Kevin was at it again.

As Doug walked back to his cubicle, he mumbled aloud to himself in frustration, *"Why does Kevin always break the copier?"*

Jan looked up from her cubicle over to Doug and asked, *"So who broke the copier? Did he break the copier? What about everyone who made copies just before him?"*

Doug came out of his slightly dazed state and looked over to Jan. He shook his head and said, *"No, it was him. He hit the print button and the copier broke. It was his fault. He caused it to break."*

Jan turned her head back down and merely said, *"Hmmm, that's interesting,"* as she looked at the Quote-of-the-Day on her calendar. It read:

The cause of a problem is never the cause.

It cannot be the cause.

The cause always has a cause which also cannot be the cause.

Reflections:

° Imagine that you have been waiting ten minutes for a co-worker to finish his 1,000-page print job at the copier. As he finishes, you place your sheet of paper on the glass and hit the print button. Two copies are made before the copier breaks. Did you break the copier?

° Are you ever blamed for things that happen in your organization that aren't really your fault?

° Do you ever blame people for things that you "know" are their fault?

(Authors' Reflections on page 186)

INQUIRY

Every year during the first week in June, the company came alive with the exuberance of youth. The college interns had arrived. This year was no different. As Javier walked down the hall, he made it a point to stop and meet each of the new faces that would disappear by August, most never to return.

Javier had sponsored internships for business undergraduates for as long as he could remember. He started this company decades ago after he finished college. But it was years later that he came to realize how his own internship experience profoundly inspired him to become a successful entrepreneur. Yes, having a college undergrad in-tow for six weeks each year slowed Javier down, but it still was his favorite time of the year. He knew this was important work.

Gina was Javier's intern this year. She was a bit surprised when she reported to Javier on the first day to ask what her duties would be. Javier simply told her, "*Come when you please and leave when you please. Wander through the organization and do as you wish. All I ask is that you meet me in my office each afternoon for a brief chat.*"

During their first meeting, it was obvious that Gina was a bit nervous. Javier asked, "*Well, what would you like to talk about?*"

Gina appeared to be at a loss for words, just as every one of his interns had been during their first meetings with him over the years. Now, most of them owned their own business and all were very successful.

Gina didn't know what to say, so Javier prodded her, "*Go ahead, Gina, you can ask me anything you want. What's on your mind?*"

At this point, Gina asked, "*What is the heart of leadership?*"

Javier smiled and responded, "*Inquiry.*"

Confused, Gina replied, *"But what do I inquire about?"*

Javier said, *"Precisely."*

Reflections:

- ° Why is inquiry essential to leadership?

- ° What should be questioned in organizations? What shouldn't?

- ° Can there ever be an end to your questioning?

- ° How do you know when you have the answers you need to be effective at work?

(Authors' Reflections on page 186)

GROUNDHOG DAY

It happens every February.

The entire division sat around the large conference room table for the end-of-year meeting. Each department head got up and made a presentation to the group on how well his or her program fared that year. Strengths, weaknesses and suggested changes for the following year were presented, reviewed, discussed and debated. The room came alive again and again as people debated the potential outcomes of yet-to-be-approved changes to programs. Notes were taken, assumptions were made and nods were given. The division vice-president was pleased, almost overwhelmed, with the level of activity and concern her team had for the success of her division. At the end of the meeting, everyone was exhausted, yet energized. Another successful year completed and a new one anticipated.

New employees to the division are usually the most eager to get involved in the discussion. They have fresh eyes and know that their input is welcome. It's also a chance for them to show everyone across the departments how bright and talented they are. Occasionally, after an end of the year review meeting, a new employee gets an idea about improving the overall effectiveness of the entire meeting.

It's always the same idea. The idea is to hold the meeting three weeks later. By delaying the meeting by just three weeks, all of the annual financial statements would be available to help evaluate the programs. After all, it is good to have hard data to review and compare the veracity of the claims made by the program managers. Everyone agrees that it is a good idea.

The following year, the meeting is held on the exact same date.

Reflections:

° Why don't leaders fix broken processes when they become known?

° How would you know if a process is broken? Would your boss agree?

° Who would benefit if the meeting time in the story changed? Who wouldn't?

° Why won't the meeting time change?

(Authors' Reflections on page 187)

RIGOR

The two consultants stood in the parking lot in front of a premier conference center in the foothills of the Rocky Mountains. Standing beside two directors of a national leadership institute, they were collectively trying to plan an upcoming three-day (and night) intensive leadership seminar for senior executives. The facility seemed to have everything – large conference rooms with majestic mountain views, a nice-sized dining facility within the main complex and extensive hiking trails adjacent to the building. It seemed perfect.

One of the directors excitedly pointed towards a thicket of scrub oak in front of the towering pine trees and started brainstorming the outdoor experiential team-building exercises he envisioned. The directors' primary objective was to create a rigorous program that challenged executives mentally, physically and emotionally. They were going to achieve this by incorporating academic content into a ropes course, hikes and a scavenger hunt. A rigorous program was expected to not only leave a lasting impression on the executives as they brought their newly acquired knowledge back to their organizations, but bind the program participants together and increase the likelihood they'd continue to network with each other long after the program was over. Rigor was key.

In fact, they decided that they wouldn't even need to make alternative plans in case of bad weather, even though the event was to take place in November. A blizzard would add to the challenge. It would increase the rigor of the program. Getting lost in white-out conditions would create a memorable experience for participants and bond them together.

As the directors stood and pondered the possibilities of adding rigor to their program, one of them realized there was, in fact, a problem with the conference center facilities. The sleeping facility wouldn't add rigor to the program. It was too nice. It wasn't luxurious, but each room had a comfortable bed, a bathroom with a shower and, God help us, a television set. TV and rigor did not belong in the same sentence. The other director immediately agreed. Such amenities would surely diminish the rigor of the program.

The two consultants really did not know what to say. They suggested that the rooms would be fine as long as the rest of the program had rigor. After all, they could exhaust the participants so thoroughly during the day that they'd be too drained to watch any late night TV. The directors thought setting up tents on the facility grounds would be better. The consultants suggested it might, however, seem strange to the participants that they would have classroom instruction in a state of the art conference center only to have to go outside to sleep in a tent at night without a place to shower. The directors paused. The lack of showers did seem to concern them. But maybe not having a shower for several days would also add to the rigor of the program.

The sleeping arrangements for the program became a major unresolved issue until one of the consultants finally pointed out, *"There's rigor. And then some things just suck."*

Reflections:

- ° How much of your job contains purposeful rigor?

- ° What elements of your job "just suck"?

- ° What can you do about those elements of your work that are painful, but don't add value?

- ° What processes do you have at work that are difficult but are essential to accomplishing your mission?

(Authors' Reflections on page 188)

THE AWARD

Judging the value of a human being can be dangerous and shouldn't be attempted. But we do it anyway. It happens in nearly every organization. We honor the best, our outstanding employees, our most valued players. We do it because we know that awards motivate people. If awards didn't work, organizations wouldn't pass them out like they do. The evidence is clear. Walk into just about anyone's office and you will find a plaque, trophy or memento to honor their accomplishments.

Most awards are accompanied with ceremony. Peers gather in a room with superiors at a head table, on a stage or at a podium. When an award winner is announced, people make noise by grunting and hitting their hands together. Perhaps with no sticks nearby, clapping is the next best thing. One might wonder how the earliest organizations honored their top performing hunters and gatherers. One has to wonder how much has changed in the last few thousand years.

No one did it better than Pendover Industries. The ceremony to crown this year's Employee of the Year was the biggest ever. The company shut down for the day and all 142 employees left their cubicles for the most luxurious hotel in the city wearing suits and ties. The food was magnificent, and the alcohol effective.

The moment everyone waited for arrived with dessert. The beloved CEO, who had an "open door policy" and meant it, took the stage to announce the year's best employee. The competition was particularly fierce this year; there was no odds-on favorite, and everyone seemed to not only have pulled their own weight, but excelled. All but a dozen or so could have been justified as the winner. That was Pendover, a great company with amazing people.

When it was announced Bill Pearson was this year's winner, there was a roar of cheers and whistles from the group. Bill was a great employee, a faithful member of his church and a fantastic dad.

Everyone loved him and it was obvious from the cheering he was a winner amongst his peers and was going places. All this occurred before the announcer read the list of Bill's accomplishments.

The week following an award ceremony was always a busy time for the CEO. He had learned to brace himself for the week ahead. Like clockwork, events unfolded just as he had expected. One after another, Pendover employees migrated towards the CEO's office and approached him with minor issues that he never would have heard about during any other week of the year. Then, after the trivial discussion about the trivial issue was over, the subordinates would all say the same basic thing:

"Oh, by the way, I probably shouldn't say anything, certainly anything negative, but did you know that Bill..."

Reflections:

  ° Do you like to win awards?

  ° Do you like to see others win awards?

  ° How do you feel when people win awards who don't deserve them? How do you know they don't deserve them?

  ° Have you deserved all the awards you've won?

  ° Can awards cause more harm than good?

(Authors' Reflections on page 189)

HEAVEN AND HELL

Kristen couldn't believe her company was serious about sending her to a new division overseas. She'd never been to the country before and only heard a few people talk about it, but that was enough. She'd decided that it was hell, a frozen hell. She had an open mind about the transfer until one of her coworkers who had spent a year there told her about the place. He advised that as soon as she gets off the plane and walks outside she'll likely get water in her ear from the strong wind blowing rain into her face. He told her not to take the water out of her ear. When Kristen asked why in the world she should leave water in her ear, her coworker smiled and said, *"It'll be in your ear the whole time you're there, you might as well get used to it. It's a rainy, windy and cold place."*

Once she arrived, she realized what people had told her about the place was true. The man she was replacing promised her a three-week overlap, but it turned out to be only two days. He said he couldn't bear to spend another day in hell.

There really was nothing there besides the company and some small towns scattered over hundreds of miles of rock. The landscape consisted mostly of rock, grass and snow and it was windy most of the time. The place didn't look like it was meant as a habitat for humans, just puffins, sea gulls, and fish.

The job was okay. It was really the same thing she had been doing in California, beautiful California. Unfortunately, Kristen couldn't separate the job from the context of living in hell. Many employees hated the place. Fortunately, most people were able to transfer out after two years. Two years in hell is a long time, though. Not everyone lasted two years.

❀ ❀ ❀ ❀ ❀ ❀

Like Kristen, Lori was also transferred overseas by her company. Unlike Kristen, Lori was thrilled. One of the reasons she loved her company was because it had divisions all over the world and it afforded her an opportunity to travel extensively. She'd never been in the country before and likely would never have gone there if it wasn't for the transfer, but she was excited about seeing what the place had to offer.

The place was cold. Not as cold as some states in the United States, but the temperature hovered around the freezing point for most of the year. In the summer it warmed up into the 60s sometimes. It was a rugged place, but it was heaven. The population of the entire country was only about 300,000 people. It probably wasn't great for city slickers, but it was paradise for anyone that loves the outdoors. It had some of the best fishing in the world. You could climb glaciers one day and bathe in hot springs the next. The people were friendly and helpful. It was an opportunity of a lifetime. The ruggedness and isolation of the place drew employees close together. They made friendships that would last forever. Unfortunately, most people had to transfer out after two years. The lucky ones found a way to stay longer.

Reflections:

° Would you consider your work environment closer to heaven or hell? By what criteria could you make this determination?

° To what extent do you create a heavenly or hellish existence for yourself?

° Describe a work environment that would be considered heaven for everyone.

° To what extent are your perceptions based on attitude and choice?

° What can you do to reframe the reality of your organizational environment in a positive light?

(Authors' Reflections on page 190)

THE BOAT

Last year, the Chief Financial Officer had asked his top performing mutual fund manager, Susan, to develop a proposal for an innovative new class of funds that would appeal to young investors of the *Millennial* generation.

Susan approached her task with exuberance. Now, moments before she would brief her proposal to the board of directors at the annual strategic planning meeting, she reflected on how well her plan turned out. Susan was both excited and proud. This was surely her best work, ever.

An hour later, as Susan walked out of the meeting, a colleague who had watched the presentation asked her, "*Well, how'd it go?*"

Susan paused for a moment and said to him, "*I was asked to produce a car and I delivered a Ferrari. People looked at it and said, 'Hmmm...I don't think it will float. Hey, Where's the sail?' It turns out they were looking for a boat. I worry we're about to build a Ferrari with a rudder.*"

Reflections:

° How often do leaders get what they ask for?

° How often do leaders get what they want?

° Should leaders ask for input from people when they already know what they want?

° If leaders don't ask, what risks do they run?

° What risks do they run if they do?

(Authors' Reflections on page 192)

THE 52ND FLOOR

"Hi, Steve. What are you working on?"

"I'm doing a report that's due tomorrow."

Squinting to see the computer screen, the first manager says, *"That looks like stuff that I'm responsible for. How come I've never seen this report? Is it something new?"*

The second manager shrugs his shoulders. *"I've been doing it for three years. I don't know who's on the distro list."*

"What do you do with it?", the first guy asks.

"I send it to the senior vice president's secretary on the 52nd floor."

"What does she do with it?"

"I have no idea."

Reflections:

° Why do so many organizations have a 52nd floor?

° How much of what you do ends up on the 52nd floor?

° What is the connection between effective leaders and 52nd floor activity?

(Authors' Reflections on page 193)

CAN YOU REALLY CREATE REALITY?

Living in the past, I have no future.

Free from the past, I have no future.

No future. No future. Same words, worlds apart.

When clients and students are asked what they think the above saying means, we get some truly wild explanations. One student actually suggested it was Hitler's guiding philosophy as he invaded Poland. Yet another suggested it was an example of a "strange loop" where one line swallows another creating a paradox defying explanation. But most people just stare at it and don't know what to say. Now it's your turn. *What do you make of this?*

Perhaps a story about our friend, Rachael, will be of some help. Several years ago, Rachael was promoted from middle management to a position in charge of "expertise." No one really knew what this position was supposed to do or why it was created. Truth be told, the position wasn't *that* new. It had actually been created two years earlier, but the guy in the job didn't do a whole lot with it. He was very smart and the *Director of Expertise* position seemed to suit him. But no one really knew what he did, and the job title offered little in way of explanation. In fact, a lot of people thought the job title was a hoax. What else could a job with a title like *Director of Expertise* be other than a Dilbert-like joke? Poor Rachael. Now the job was hers.

It wasn't long after Rachael had taken over her new position that people slowly started to realize the "expertise" function was no hoax and certainly no joke. As issues occurred in the company, Rachael started addressing them in staff meetings. It became quite routine to find her walking into a colleague's office and saying, *"There is a problem in your department and as the Director of Expertise it falls in my area of responsibility. How do you think we should address it?"* It happened so slowly and unobtrusively that no one in the organization realized what was happening. Within six months, it seemed as if Rachael was running the entire organization.

Rachael certainly could have done exactly what her predecessor had done. She could have adopted her predecessor's conception of the job and enacted the past into the future. Rachael didn't do that. Instead, she chose to create something which did not previously exist. There was no predetermined past enacting a predetermined future. For her, the future was malleable...it didn't exist until *she* created it.

So consider where you stand. Are you living in the past or are you free from your past? To the extent either are true, what do you see transpiring in your future?

We fully recognize this final passage likely doesn't make much sense to some people when they initially encounter it. And that's okay. Thinking deeply is hard and our natural inclination is to fight against it. We must resist the urge. How much can we really appreciate answers when they are merely handed to us? Could a business be sustainable if it didn't create anything?

Is being a leader any different?

AUTHORS' REFLECTIONS...*On Understanding*

Relationships (p.166)

A relationship is a constant exchange between two parties. People do not really have relationships with organizations. Organizations, while structured through policies and processes do not and cannot perceive the exchange, and therefore are not in the relationship. It is the people who collectively breathe life into an organization creating the sense of it being a living entity.

Nevertheless, some organizations take on a life of their own. From an objective point of view, organizations consist of people and "stuff," such as buildings, equipment, and raw materials. The stuff has no meaning outside of the people who work with it. It is easy for us to lose sight of this and think organizations are entities outside of the people who give life to them. This is a mistake. When this happens, organizations get into trouble. We should never forget that organizations are people, for people. What truly defines an organization is purpose.

Why does the organization exist? Whose needs does it serve? The customers have needs. They desire the organization's product or service. The stakeholders have needs. Shareholders want to maximize their stock value. Bondholders want the organization to successfully repay the money it borrowed. Employees desire the income stream, the social discussion around the water cooler and, of course, matching contributions to the 401(k). Then there are the leaders, executives, generals or elected officials. They have needs, too, and that's the point. Organizations are need-based in much the same way relationships are. Human beings have an innate desire to be needed, to be validated, to be involved. These needs are motivated in the pursuit of some purpose. Organizations could not exist if not for human needs and purposes. We should look at *purpose and relationships* before *problems and causes*. Within a system, everything is related to everything else, even if it might not appear that way. This cannot be overemphasized.

Feedback (p.167)

Most of us recognize the importance of feedback, but we are constantly surprised so few people actually want *real feedback*. We've come to understand nearly everyone wants validation and positive feedback, but few truly desire negative feedback which is so critical to growth and improvement. To make matters worse, it is rare to find people willing to *give* negative feedback, even to the few people who actually want it. No wonder all of our leaders think they're above average.

We have dealt a great deal with military organizations and the story below remains among our favorites to share.

> Within the military domain, generals don't typically talk to junior officers any more than CEOs talk to shift supervisors. So it came as a surprise one afternoon when I looked up and saw a three-star general standing in my doorway. Never before had I seen such a high-ranking person in our building, certainly not on our floor and never in my office. I stood up and said, *"To what do I owe this pleasure, General?"*
>
> The general smiled and said," *I want some feedback."*
>
> All the alarm bells in my head went off. This could be a disaster. I swallowed hard knowing I might regret what I was about to say, but I said it anyway:
>
> *"In all due respect, General, I'm not sure what I just heard. In my experience, when senior executives ask for feedback, what they are really searching for is validation. Thus, I'm not sure what you want me to tell you."*

> *"May I please sit down?"* said the general. Pulling up a chair, he looked at me with a very warm smile and said,*" You know, you're right. My experience has taught me the same thing. Most senior officers are typically looking to be told 'what a great job they are doing' when they ask for 'feedback.' But I really mean it. I need some feedback and I understand you are the one I can really get it from."*

The rest of the story is unimportant, but the point is clear. When leaders ask for feedback, you have to ask yourself, *"what do they really want?"*

The Cause (p.168)

We tend to overlook the most obvious cause of common problems we observe because we focus to the *second closest* cause. It's like reading with your nose too close to the book – you can see shades of black and white, but it is hard to make sense of the letters and words. When you take a step back and look at the situation objectively, you might notice that you could have something to do with the problem. Could *you* be the *cause*? We could always point to a deeper level cause and ultimately say the system was the cause of all events that occur. But who created the system?

Inquiry (p.170)

The heart of leadership is constant inquiry. Yet, we rarely know what to inquire about. To inquire with the right attitude and with humility can launch novices and old hats alike on a continuing journey of leadership.

Some people are quite content coming home each day at 5:00 p.m., eating dinner, reading the paper and watching some television. On the weekend, the grass is cut, the laundry is washed and the ball game is watched. During the two-week summer vacation, relatives are visited. Routines are comfortable because of the illusion of certitude they provide. For some, this is what they seek.

There is another group of people who never seem to be satisfied with what they know. They have a constant desire to seek a better understanding of themselves and the world in which they live. They recognize at a deep level, they may never have sought to understand so many things which had been taken for granted. For them, learning is part of their identity. Constant inquiry isn't a strategy; it is a way of life. As leaders, we need to understand both groups of people exist and manage accordingly.

Groundhog Day (p.172)

Over the years, we've discovered when faulty and antiquated processes, which somehow seem to be serving powerful players in the organization are questioned or challenged by people in an organization, the issue should be dealt with cautiously. Leaders who have worked their way up the corporate ladder are generally quite intelligent and are just as capable of seeing flaws in their organization as the rest of us. The fact they haven't fixed obvious stovepipes or eliminated unnecessary policies may likely reveal something about who benefits from the status quo.

Regardless of what people might believe the meeting does or doesn't do, what is undeniable is how meetings have an innate way of exposing people's true identities which aren't always apparent. Take for example a very senior associate who had a reputation for being laid back and pleasant. Once a year, at the meeting in the Groundhog Day story, he became the "bulldog." Just like every other year before, people were "surprised."

Meetings allow people in the organization to better understand the less obvious aspects of the office dynamics. When the meeting is finally over, there is a lot of self-congratulating for "a job well done." As they say in Hollywood, *"no publicity is bad publicity."* If there is an organizational corollary, it's *"all professional communication in an organization is valuable communication."* It is another venue for us to better understand the complex and oftentimes ambiguous environment in which we operate.

Maybe no meeting is a complete waste of time. Think of it as a scene of a play – as organizational theater. Each meeting acts as a stage for elaborate dramatic productions. If this is true, then the purpose of the meeting would merely be a cloak for the real agenda, which would likely have its roots in the motivations of the "lead actor." Some might look for voice, others for affirmation, and still others for an audience.

Rigor (p.174)

"It builds character."

Huh? That's right. All too often, employees confess they have aspects of their jobs which are simply unpleasant. Some aspects of "pain" are justified. If you are a public safety servant, say a fire fighter, police officer or a sheriff's deputy, you are going to have periods of extreme boredom and others of sheer terror. That's just the nature of the job. But all too often, many leaders seem to believe it is necessary to practice enduring pain so when you have to endure it, you are prepared. Sounds bizarre, we know, but it happens all the time.

You wouldn't think it would happen in an administrative setting, but think again. A junior associate is asked to prepare a report. It's due quarterly, but the boss asks for it monthly. The report takes 8-12 hours to compile. The boss knows this, but when questioned about it, he told us *"It's good for him. Helps get him ready for the days ahead when he really has a lot to do."*

Rigor should be a natural condition of necessity, never a designed condition. From necessity emerges effort and vigor; from design, cynicism and malcontent.

Rigor, like anything else transpiring in an organizational domain needs to have a purpose. Unless such purpose is strictly attributable to the organization's goals or mission, it should be questioned. Comments such as, "*That's the way it's always been done*" or "*That's what I had to do when I did that job*" are telling. The old adage "no pain, no gain" is simply wrong. Good leaders follow a tried and true dictum: "No pain, no pain." It actually works.

The Award (p.176)

Human beings are naturally inclined to take credit for success ("*I'm so talented!*") and blame their shortcomings on things beyond their control ("*These things just happen.*") Perhaps this wouldn't be problematic if we were consistent. But we're not. In fact, we tend to reverse this arrangement when we view others. We tend to attribute their success to the situation (or luck) and their shortcomings to a lack of talent or effort. Add all this up and virtually any award will violate someone's perception of equity. Funny thing is, if you do away with awards, you may violate everyone's sense of equity. In the language of academicians, it is referred to as "the fundamental attribution error." Truly, it is fundamental. You see it all the time in organizations.

Award programs are commonly believed to be a necessary part of every organization. They are commonly believed to be a *win-win* proposition. The boss gets to recognize superior performance and show his commitment to standards and awareness of employee effort. The employee getting the award feels validated and gets the well-needed boost in self-esteem. Everyone else gets to share in the joy of the ceremony where his or her colleagues are recognized. Awards are a good motivator for everyone, or at least this is the conventional wisdom.

We see it a bit differently. It actually works like this:

(1) The boss presents Bill with the award.

(2) Half the people in attendance are thinking, "*Bill didn't deserve that award. If anyone, it was Bob!*

Bob out-performed Bill at every turn. This award isn't fair."

(3) The other half of the room is thinking, *"Bill didn't deserve that award, I did. This award isn't fair."*

(4) The boss is thinking, *"I think I'll take tomorrow afternoon off and play a little golf."*

(5) Bill is thinking, *"I'm the man!' Awards are never fair in this organization. It's good to see they finally got it right!"*

Awards have the potential to wreak havoc in an organization. Don't let the smiles and applause fool you.

Heaven and Hell (p.178)

We create our realities in two major ways. First, we create our filters, our attitudes and our world views which, in turn, create the unique perspective we apply to our world. Second, we enact our perspective by altering the perspectives of others. There is a complex interaction between our perspectives and how we bring them to bear. The power here lies in the fact we never have to accept another's reality, or even our own reality, at any given time. We can turn what we consider an organization on a downward spiral into a success by understanding our ability to create reality for ourselves and others. The possibilities are limitless. We can change the world by changing ourselves and the way we choose to see it.

Change. We hear it all the time: "The only constant factor in organizations is change." Leaders who develop the adaptive capacity to embrace the ambiguity created by change will always be in demand to the people and organizations that rely on them. How can we develop our own adaptive capacity? Practice. We all face change in our lives. How we react to it is a choice.

Take for example a story of a man who had nearly spent his entire adult life in the town in which he grew up. He married his high school sweetheart, got a dog and built a house with a white-picket fence. He had the perfect job, the perfect life. And then one day, his organization decided to transfer him to another part of the country – far, far away from all that he knew. As the news began to sink in, he started to think about what this change would mean for life as he knew it. He would have to leave the job he loved. His wife would have to quit hers. The kids would have to sever the only childhood friendships they had ever known. The grandparents would no longer see the grandkids on a weekly basis. He was devastated. This was completely unexpected news, and there was no getting around it. *"How am I going to break the news to my family?"* he wondered. And then it hit him.

As he walked into the house, he smiled. His wife asked, *"Wow, you're in a good mood. Did you have a good day at the office?"* He replied, *"It was great! I found out we got an all-expense-paid vacation for the next few years to another state! What an incredible opportunity!"*

It was at that moment the screaming began.

A year after the move, a former colleague visited his friend at his new home and asked:

"So how does your family like living here?"

"We love it," he replied.

"Really?", said the friend.

"Yes, in fact, just last week I joked with the children the organization wants me back at my old job and we might move again. When they heard this, they immediately turned on me and said, 'But Dad, no! Please, no! We love it here.'"

Life is indeed all about the choices we make. As the classic wisdom goes, if you really want to be happy in life, then you must be happy today. The way leaders see, and choose *to be*, is a choice…and it matters.

The Boat (p.180)

We *all* need feedback, but is feedback *always* necessary? Many of us want to include as many people as possible in the decision-making processes. *But do we really need to?* As leaders, we sometimes need to be reminded our primary job is to make decisions for the organization, but all decisions are not created equally. Some decisions may require input from everyone. A good example would be the development of the office parking plan or the allocation of window offices. In the absence of clearly pre-established rules, such decisions can be highly contentious. Allowing everyone to have a voice can go a long way towards creating a sense of equity in the outcome. Since a plan developed in isolation would likely be judged as "unfair" by some, maximal participation is essential.

When it comes to more critical matters, however, such as dealing with budget expenditures, project selection or strategic development, the leader's vision is critical in shaping the future growth and development of the organization. Because others in the organization may have very different motivations, agendas or perspectives conflicting with a leader's vision, soliciting input could backfire. *If feedback is not needed, but a leader asks for it anyway, what will happen?* The leader will get it, of course, but once received, usually, one of two situations occur.

First, if the feedback is not really wanted, the leader is now faced with creating a perception that "the boss doesn't care what we think" if the feedback is not used. From then on, people may be more wary of giving their input if they believe the leader is insincere and never wanted input from the beginning. Soliciting unwanted input can create a barrier to effective communication for the leader in the future when feedback might really be valued.

Second, by asking for input and getting input which conflicts with a leader's envisioned future, the leader may be forced to a compromise resulting in an outcome which appeases many, satisfies no one and worse, creates little or no value. In the end, everyone loses.

We might not see many Ferraris with rudders driving down the road, but unfortunately we see many similar compromises emerge from strategic planning sessions where leaders are less direct than they should have been. Sometimes, directness may be exactly what your team needs.

The 52nd Floor (p.181)

Bureaucracy and process are essential to structure organizational communication. Otherwise, as soon as an organization expanded beyond a handful of employees, it would be hard to regulate the flow of information. Thus, organizations organize. That's kind of the point, right? It becomes necessary to organize people, data and resources and regulate how organizations should interact internally. Almost inevitably, a 52nd floor emerges.

Many leaders are unaware they have a 52nd floor in their organization. They have no idea when they make a casual statement for someone to "*look into this*" or "*consider the feasibility of that*" they may have just issued an edict from the 52nd floor.

Strategic planning is a great example. If you've ever been part of a team that's been charged with writing such a plan, you know what we mean. Hours, weeks, months are spent creating a document covering all aspects of the organization, its capabilities, an environmental assessment and on and on. After many months, the plan is finally complete. This masterpiece represents the best efforts of some of the most talented and highly paid people in the organization. Great care is taken to bind it and print it in color, complete with abstracts and executive summaries.

When we visit with clients, we often ask senior executives to tell us about their strategic planning process. More often than not, this seems to be a source of pride for them.

That is, until we ask :

"When was the last time you actually read, or even saw for that matter, a copy of your strategic plan?" (Pause)

"Do you know where a copy of it is?" (Pause)

"How many times in the last year have you referred to your strategic plan in making key strategic decisions for the organization?" (Silence)

Surprisingly, fewer than 50% of executives can readily access a copy of their organization's strategic plan and far fewer have even opened it in the course of making any strategic decisions. Many of these plans are filed on the 52nd floor. This doesn't mean the process to develop the plan didn't create value for the organization. It might, however, call into question how much value really emerges from such a process. It is probably far less than most leaders care to admit.

When you find yourself doing something for the 52nd floor, or worse, asking someone else who works for you to do something of the sort, pause for a moment and consider what purpose is to be achieved, what value is to be gained, what costs might be incurred?

Tasks destined for the 52nd floor demand inquiry. *Ask questions. Ask the right questions.* Effective leadership is grounded in purpose – the organization has a purpose – leaders have a purpose – employees have a purpose. Your purpose, regardless of your leadership role, is to seek a greater understanding of the complex interrelationships within the organization you are leading.

We considered many potential titles for this book, but *The 52nd Floor* seemed to stick. When people heard the title, they immediately started *asking questions!* Questions such as *"What does the 52nd Floor mean?"* or *"What goes on all the way up there?"* It didn't matter what the questions were, but rather that the title *invited questions.* We believe this to be one of the greatest lessons for leaders to grasp: *asking questions – the right questions –* is essential.

THE JOURNEY'S END
A NEW BEGINNING

"If I had some set idea of a finish line, don't you think I would have crossed it years ago?" —Bill Gates

---

And a final story...

HEY PROFESSOR

"Hey professor, do you have any good stories for us today?"

"Well, it should be a pretty good show. It just depends..."

"Depends on what?"asks the student.

"It depends on whether or not you're willing to do the work."

"What work? We just answer your questions and talk about your stories."

"That's the work. The show's only as good as your willingness to answer my questions. You are the show."

Reflection:

° How is the approach used in this book different from other "leadership books" you have encountered?

In 2008, Professor Emeritus Jim Heskett published a commentary in *Working Knowledge* entitled "*Why Don't Managers Think Deeply?*"[1] He described a former colleague who used to routinely sit on a bench outside the Harvard Business School and "*stare off into space.*" Sitting amidst some of the most highly educated and motivated people in the world, this behavior attracted the attention of many. When approached and asked if something was wrong, he would merely smile and indicate he was fine. But to the casual observer, his behavior wasn't *normal*. Business school professors are trained to admire and teach action. What sense could be made of an elder professor just sitting? Many might have assumed he was doing nothing. However, we believe he may have been engaged in deliberate practice of one of the most valuable skills leaders could ever hope to master: the art of thinking deeply.

So why is it the acts of sitting, thinking and reflecting are often viewed by others as being lazy, unproductive or odd? Perhaps it's because we have learned from our earliest experiences in school and organizational life to *do things*. We don't wish to insinuate that common intuition is wrong. On the contrary, we routinely observe those who are the most productive, diligent and active as achieving the highest levels of success. We have learned action leads to success, but from where will the big ideas emerge? How will we know if we are making good decisions until we are able to observe the products of our action? *Is there value to leaders who pause, step back and reflect?* Professor Heskett believed it was no coincidence some of the most profound insights uttered at faculty meetings came from his quiet, reflective colleague. If leaders are to have vision and insight when they "reach the top" but are promoted up the ranks on their ability to get things done, is it possible to become both a deep thinker and a high achiever simultaneously?

We believe thinking deeply is a skill which can be learned while doing other action-oriented activities. While many of us may not have the luxury of sitting on a park bench to think and reflect, just about everyone has the time to read and reflect. But is that it?

Read and reflect? We can become deep thinkers by reading and reflecting?

Yes. We believe you can. Just like the skill that is required to juggle or play the piano, developing the skill for deep thinking takes practice. We must read great books – books that stimulate our thinking, books that question our assumptions, books that make us think. We must take time out of our busy lives to practice this skill. No concert pianist could achieve such a level of success without deliberate practice. We believe the same dictum holds true for leaders. To develop great skill at influencing others, leaders practice by doing it along with thinking deeply about it.

The standards to which we hold our leaders are a bit unfair. We often expect them to have the answers and to make sense of the intricacies of organizational life. We do not claim the topics we have covered in this book are exhaustive, nor do we claim they are the most important. We do, believe, however, based on our years of experience working with so many leaders in industry, government and small business, the journeys in this book are essential building blocks for success.

In the *Journey Into Leadership*, we wanted to show how a fascination with "what is leadership" often leads to wrong questions and dead ends. Whether or not leadership exists might be an interesting academic debate, but leaders need to "deliver the goods." *What do leaders do?* They influence others, they listen and they work to be the type of leader their followers need them to be. *How do they do this?* They create it. They create the images, beliefs and perceptions in the minds of others to enact the social reality necessary to unify and catalyze action toward a shared and desired goal. Using stories, we hoped to demonstrate some of these lessons.

The *Journey Into Power* attempted to illustrate how leaders can create dependencies with others to influence action. Although there are arguably many different types of power, leaders have tremendous opportunities every day to create dependent relationships with colleagues, superiors, subordinates, suppliers, stakeholders – anyone – to better influence them to act as the leader desires. Power creates action.

In the *Journey Into Human Behavior*, we discussed the highly complex set of thought processes, rationale and emotions which routinely challenge a leader's abilities to influence others. Leaders have to be mindful of how others view the world. What motivates the leader may not motivate others. Going on an early morning "fun run" might not motivate an office full of out-of-shape middle-aged folks. The same holds true for a "morale dinner" on a Saturday afternoon when some people will need to get baby-sitters and others will miss college football. If leaders hope to motivate their constituents, then they must get to know their people and figure out what truly motivates them to become the type of followers the leader desires.

We tried to illustrate in a *Journey Into Culture* how powerful creating the right type of organizational climate and culture can be in controlling behavior. The astute leader works to create the correct set of stimuli to bring out the deeply held values and beliefs of their followers and uses these values to bring together the diversity of individuals and their ideas to work toward a common cause. Some experts believe if a leader only tends to the organizational culture, the rest of the organization will take care of itself. Although this statement might be a bit guilty of oversimplifying the art of leadership, it is probably more correct than not.

As we ventured on to the *Journey Into Control*, we hoped to show the very different approaches leaders could take to control the behavior of their followers. On one hand, leaders can attempt to control individual actions of followers and their organization. However, trying too hard to control aspects of behavior may have negative impacts on the organization's climate and culture because it overlooks the critical factors that motivate people. Although it may seem trivial, creating a culture based on trust, inclusion and mutual respect may be the surest way for a leader to gain and maintain control of followers while simultaneously creating the desired organizational climate which, over time, will shape the organization's culture.

We ended our journey with several stories in the *Journey Into Understanding* which touched on multiple areas of the book, but all highlighted a common theme – enactment. For a leader to be successful, he or she must continuously think deeply and reflect on both *what he knows* and *how he know what he knows*. Yes, the leader must dedicate himself or herself to a life of learning and inquiry to better understand the ever-changing, ambiguous environment in which he or she lives. Followers will look to their leaders for guidance and when they do, the leaders must be ready, willing and able to enact the reality they envision.

In closing, we left you with one of our favorite stories, *Hey Professor*, because it helps remind us of the most important aspect of leadership – it is up to the leader to create and enact the social reality within their organization.

The 52nd Floor: Thinking Deeply About Leadership is a call to write and act in your own production.

We hope you put on a really good show.

EPILOGUE

The Red Stapler Club

Some people get up in the morning and go to work in their cubicle. Others spring out of bed and can't wait to get to the office. Indeed, the latter group is small, but it does exist. For them, going to "work" feels like a home away from home. What makes the culture of an organization so infectious it creates an innate desire for employees to be around one another? In this case, it was red staplers.

There was no time clock to punch. The workday started at 7:30 a.m. Everyone knew it and yet no one seemed to care. Many people had already been working for the past hour and a half. Others probably wouldn't saunter in for another hour or so. No one really even paid attention to when people came and went. Everyone knew that everyone else was committed to adding as much value to the organization as they could on a daily basis. To the outside observer, it seemed like a stereotypical office environment. Nothing could have been further from the truth.

You could always tell when the lunch gathering had begun, because the laughter and chatter would fill the back halls of the office. It was typical for someone, anyone really, to walk around to all of the offices and say, *"Come on, it's lunch time"* and moments later a stream of folks carrying everything from a Tupperware dish with leftovers to a baggie of bean sprouts would be heading to the back.

Randy probably looked forward to lunchtime with his colleagues more than anyone else. He always took it upon himself to make sure everyone knew the noontime festivities had begun. But on this particular day, he was the last one out of his office, except he didn't realize it. He had been in a meeting and wasn't interrupted.

As he walked to the lunchroom, peering into all the offices and finding them vacant, he noticed something. Two of his colleagues had red staplers. His was black. How could he not have noticed this before? One of his favorite movies was *Office Space,* and these were exact replicas of Milton's stapler. That's right, the Swingline Model 747™ – the King of Staplers. The prominent display of these iconic artifacts made him wonder how he had not noticed them before.

Randy seemed to have forgotten about lunch. He started going from office to office to see if anyone else had a red stapler. *Holy smokes!* Fourteen of the forty offices had a red stapler. And his was not one of them.

There was something going on. The fact that fourteen people *had* red staplers and twenty-six *didn't* meant something. Clearly, Randy had been left out. So, liking a good practical joke now and then and feeling a little more than mischievous, Randy decided to have some fun.

Early the next morning, before the arrival of the early birds, Randy went around to every office that did not have a red stapler and posted a sign. The sign was simple:

Randy then left the building to later return at his normal arrival time. When Randy arrived nearly an hour later, people in the division were actively engaged in discovering the meaning behind the signs. *"What does it mean?" "Why do I have one and you do not?" "Is there a pattern?"*

Several people came by Randy's office that morning and commented on the fact he was one of the office members who had a sign posted on his door. The questions were the same: *"Do you know what it means?" "Who do you think is behind this?"* Randy simply shrugged his shoulders and feigned his own curiosity, *"Who's John Galt?"*

Needless to say, the secret signs dominated the lunch conversations. One trio had even compiled a list of the *haves* and *have nots* in hopes of discerning a pattern. They reported that although the department head had not been tagged, her deputy had been. Even someone's fish tank had been tagged. Several of the most senior members of the department were tagged, but so were some of the "newbies" in the office. It just didn't make sense. Conversation in the lunchroom soon morphed from *"Who did it"* to *"What does 'RSC' mean?"*

This continued for nearly two weeks. Randy secretly enjoyed playing along and watching all of the organizational sleuths working to solve the RSC mystery. As Randy reflected on all of the fun the department was having over this trivial mystery, it caused him to reflect on just how much he loved working there. The work they did was important work – work that made you feel as though you were making a difference. But as much as the work, it was the people. They were like a family. Of course, there were the occasional conflicts, but as in any family, they were always resolved for the good of the family.

More importantly, Randy had made some dear friends during his time in the division. The kind of friends you have for life. Randy also felt he had never been a part of such a talented group as this, and likely never would be again.

Then it happened. Randy came back from a meeting one morning to find a brand-new red stapler on his desk with a note from Kurt, one of his colleagues. The note read, "*All you had to do was ask.*"

Randy's initial inclination was correct. There *was* something to the coveted red staplers!

Someone had finally solved his RSC puzzle, but now Randy was once again in the dark. "*What do these staplers mean?*" he wondered, and "*Why from Kurt?*"Randy couldn't take the mystery anymore. Now that he knew Kurt was behind this "conspiracy," he went straight to Kurt's office.

Kurt was waiting for him, sitting at his desk, smiling, with his own red stapler prominently displayed. Without prompting, Kurt began to explain:

> "*After I saw the movie* Office Space, *I spotted this stapler in a store and just had to buy it. I brought it to work and immediately had people commenting on it. So I decided to order a case of them and give them out to anyone who appreciated the stapler and its Milton connection. All you had to do was ask.*"

> "*But you do realize very soon, the word will be out and* everyone *in the office will want one, so could you help with the cost of ordering another case?*" finished Kurt.

All Randy could do was smile back and say, "*Touché.*"

* * * * * *

Later that day, Kurt sent out a division-wide e-mail that read as follows:

Dear Colleagues,

Many of you have seen the letters "RSC" appearing throughout the department over the last several weeks. This TLA (three-letter acronym) stimulated much analysis and scholarly debate. As it turns out, the story is *Relatively Simple to Clarify (RSC)*.

Several weeks ago, Randy walked around the department to get a feel for our norms, symbols, and informal structure. This is always a great way to *Recognize Systems and Culture (RSC)* in an organization. Among other things, Randy noticed that some members of the faculty had red staplers and others did not. This interesting cultural artifact was articulated by Randy as the *Red Stapler Club (RSC)*. The red stapler was made famous in the movie *Office Space* by a character named Milton. As it turns out, Milton has been fired but continued to show up at the office, do meaningless work, and receive a paycheck (sound familiar?). Milton clings to his red stapler as one last vestige of personal dignity against a system that cares little about him or the humanity of its workers.

Given the *Rich Symbolic Connotation (RSC)* of the red stapler and its appeal to the common worker in all of us, red staplers are now available for anyone who wants one. Just send me an e-mail or stop by my office to pick one up free of charge. This opportunity for each of us to have a free red stapler is possible because of the willingness of *Randy to Spend Cash (RSC)* to make his dream of a *Red Stapler Culture (RSC)* a reality in DFM. Please let me know if you would like one of these very special red Swingline Model 747 staplers and please thank Randy for making this a place with *Really Special Colleagues (RSC)*!

Thanks,

Kurt

Before long, everyone in the division had a red stapler. But the red stapler no longer symbolized a connection to a movie, but rather the employees' connections to each other. Years later, people who left the organization and returned to visit former colleagues would inevitably remark about how they continue to prominently display their red stapler as a symbol of one of the most positive and effective organizational cultures they had ever known.

The following year, Randy was packing up his office. Advancing to positions of greater responsibility was always bittersweet for anyone in the division. He lamented what a shame there wasn't an organization which could capture the magic of such a group of amazing people outside the traditional organizational boundaries. He imagined a new organization that would keep people connected. It could be for-profit or non-profit, it could be a business venture or merely a think tank. Regardless of what the organization ultimately might become, it would connect exceptionally talented people to add immense value to those they served.

As for the group's name, that would be easy. They'd call it RSC.

www.rscgroup.org

POSTSCRIPT

Although there are far too many people to name and thank for an endeavor such as this, we feel compelled to acknowledge our former students. Words cannot accurately articulate the pride, respect and admiration we have for each of you.

We owe an equal debt of gratitude to the faculty and staff of the Department of Management at the U.S. Air Force Academy. We will forever cherish the opportunity we had to work with such a high-caliber group of individuals who exemplified the qualities of passion, inquiry, competence and integrity. Your influence on us profoundly impacted many of the perspectives shared in this manuscript.

We would also be remiss if we didn't especially credit three individuals for their profound influence on this book. The first is Kevin Davis. But for him, there would be no book. Second is Kurt Heppard ("Dr. Z" from *Ladies and Gentlemen*). Without him, there never would have been a *Red Stapler Club*. Thanks also to Kurt for suggesting the title and allowing us to use it. Last, we wish to express our heartfelt thanks to Steve Green for two decades of unwavering encouragement and support.

Finally, we want to thank Enso's editors and staff – Abbie, Harry, Tomma, Narinder and Jon – for their tenacious dedication and support from start to finish. Likewise, our most sincere appreciation goes to the following reviewers who took the time to provide exceptionally thorough critiques and feedback. In alphabetical order, they are Andy Armacost, Nathan Atherley, Jim Barker, Jeff Butler, Lise Diez-Arguelles, Steve Fraser, Kari Granger, Paul Hoffman, Rich Hughes, Rob Mishev, Michael J.C. Roth, Joe Sanders in addition to two anonymous reviewers. Your comments and suggestions went a long way into making the book into what it is.

Although the credit is to be shared with so many, all errors and omissions are entirely our own.

---∞∞∞---

APPENDIX A
STANDING ON THE SHOULDERS OF GIANTS

In the process of writing this book, we remained mindful that ideas do not emerge in isolation. Every aspect of this book is an amalgam of published works, personal experiences, and dialogue. Although it is impossible to trace any concept down to the original source, we would be remiss if we didn't acknowledge some of the *intellectual giants* who have inspired our thinking over the years. While this section is only intended to highlight some of their more salient works, additional bibliographic citations can be found in the *Notes* section.

A Journey Into Leadership

The Myth of Leadership – Pfeffer

Jeffrey Pfeffer led the earliest scholarly inquiry into the very nature and existence of leadership as a verifiable construct. He questioned whether or not leadership matters as much as people commonly believe it does. Pfeffer suggested that much of what we think we know about leadership may be nothing more than our own attributional processes at work, relegating leadership to a myth we have created to simplify our individual perception of events and their causes.

Pfeffer, J. (1994). *Managing with Power: Politics and Influence in Organizations*. Boston, MA: Harvard Business School Press.

Leadership Theory – Yukl

Gary Yukl's *Leadership in Organizations* is a necessary starting point for anyone wishing to learn more "about leadership." Yukl's book has become the standard reference for practitioners, researchers, and educators alike. His comprehensive review of leadership theories and research is focused towards answering the illusive question, "What makes someone an effective leader?"

Yukl, G.A. (2005). *Leadership in Organizations*. 6th Edition. New York, NY: Prentice-Hall.

❀ *Stewardship – Block*

Peter Block's perspective on choosing service over self-interest is a recurring theme in our stories and reflections. The notion of stewardship suggests that leaders essentially need to be accountable without taking control. This approach can generate an emergent self-governing force. Block contends that stewardship honors the responsibility given to leaders by using their power with compassion and grace to pursue purposes that transcend short-term self-interest.

Block, Peter. (1993). *Stewardship: Choosing Service Over Self Interest*. San Francisco, CA: Berrett-Koehler.

❀ *Political Leadership – Ferris*

Gerald Ferris and colleagues developed a sophisticated perspective of leadership that implies effective leaders are politically astute individuals who have a great capacity to influence others. His perspective discounts the common belief that leaders use their political skill to pursue personal ambitions or to manipulate others. Instead, he believes political skill may be one of the most important attributes of successful leaders. Ferris identifies political skill as it is an integrated composite of internally consistent and mutually reinforcing abilities that create a synergistic social dynamic.

Ferris, G. R. , Davidson, S.L, & Perrewe, P.L. (2005). *Political Skill at Work: Impact on Work Effectiveness*. Mountain View, CA: Davies-Black.

A Journey Into Power

ᙡᙠ *Bases of Social Power – French and Raven*

The significance of French and Raven's work cannot be overstated. Virtually all discussions on power start with French and Raven's perspective – ours included. French and Raven's suggested there are five bases of power: reward, coercive, legitimate, referent and expert. They define reward power as the discretionary ability to grant a positive outcome while coercive power is the ability to impose a negative outcome. Legitimate power invokes an *ought- ness* in followers obligating others' compliance. Referent power is the ability to influence due to social desirability or attraction, and finally, expert power is derived from the perception of the relative and relevant knowledge one has to another.

French, J.R.P., & Raven, B. (1959). 'The bases of social power,' in D. Cartwright (ed.) *Studies in Social Power.* Ann Arbor, MI: University of Michigan Press.

ᙡᙠ *Dependencies – Maslow*

Abraham Maslow's renowned hierarchy of needs continues to be a mainstay in social psychology despite widespread criticism and lack of empirical support. Its popularity is likely due to the fact that it just seems to make sense. While we don't necessarily agree with all of Maslow's assertions, we can't deny the impact that his hierarchy of needs has had on us. When we view power, we assert that all power can be viewed as needs or dependencies.

Maslow, A. H. (1998). *Toward a Psychology of Being.* 3rd Edition. San Francisco, CA: Wiley.

ᙡᙠ *Power and Dependence – Emerson*

Richard Emerson advanced a theory of power revolving around the ties of mutual dependence that bind individuals togeth- er in social systems. Emerson was the first to suggest that power was not a possession. He suggested that ties of mutual dependence imply that each party is in a position, to some degree, to grant or deny, facilitate or hinder the other's gratification. Emerson also suggested that we manage balancing operations in order to mitigate the effects of power inequity.

Emerson, R.M. (1962). Power-Dependence Relationships. *American Sociological Review, 27,* 31-43.

❧ *Interdependencies – Kotter*

John Kotter contends power is imbedded in interdependencies that exist in relationships. The greater the dependence, the more important the relationship. He presented the organization as an increasingly complex social milieu imbedded with intricate patterns of interdependencies which place an ever-burgeoning premium on leaders that understand power and influence.

Kotter, J. P. (1985). *Power and Influence.* New York, NY: Free Press.

❧ *Trust and Social Exchange – Ensminger*

Ensminger's anthropological fieldwork in the Tana River District in Kenya illuminates how trust relationships evolved as the most efficient and least costly means of control in the region. Advancing her argument that trust reduces these costs, Ensminger describes how cattle owners and herders develop relationships based on reciprocity. She points to the paternal adoption of trustworthy herders by owners as evidence of this argument. This is the result of an iterative process that grows in opportunity costs for both the owner and the herder the longer the relationship exists. For the herder, the cost of shirking may result in starting over with a new owner at a lower wage level. For the owner, losses for defaulting on a relationship are exceedingly high.

Ensminger, J. (1996). *Making a Market: The Institutional Transformation of an African Society.* Cambridge, MA: Cambridge Press.

A Journey Into Human Nature

❊ *Dramaturgy and Self-Presentation – Goffman*

According to Erving Goffman, a social scientist who first introduced the notion of self-presentation as a form of drama, the self is the product of the scene acted out and not the cause of the scene. The self is not some "Oz" behind a curtain deciding what and in which scene to act and what the script will be. Rather, it is the collective perception of the role played. This suggests that the self is as much a product of our social surroundings as it is a product of our own design. As we adjust our behavior to be "appropriate" for a certain situation, we are presenting a different version of ourselves and at least some of that presentation is defined by the social situation. Having multiple-selves dramatically (no pun intended) different from each other creates the risk of diluting any sense of *real self*. This can be perceived by others as being insincere and inconsistent in our performance.

Goffman, E. (1959). *The Presentation of Self in Everyday Life.* Norwell, MA: Anchor.

❊ *Self – Gergen*

Kenneth Gergen claims that we experience multiphrenia (i.e. social saturation) when we split the individual into a multiplicity of selves. Once created, these self-investments compete for our time and attention, thereby causing a dilution, and potentially, dissolution of the self. He warns us to be careful not to be too many things to too many people. The potential costs are measured in terms of an erosion of perceived sincerity as well as personal tolls.

Gergen, K.J. (2000). *The Saturated Self: Dilemmas of Identity in Everyday Life.* New York, NY: Basic Books.

✿ *Role-Sets – Katz and Kahn*

In *The Social Psychology of Organizations,* Daniel Katz and Robert Kahn portray organizational members as belonging to role-sets. They suggest that these role-sets constantly evolve as we continuously negotiate who is in a particular role-set and what behaviors are expected from it. Roles become a source of conflict as our different roles demand behaviors that are inconsistent with the other roles in our lives. Additionally, a significant source of stress can result when we face ambiguous role expectations.

Katz, K. & Kahn, R.L. (1978). *The Social Psychology of Organizations.* Hoboken, NJ: Wiley.

✿ *Integral Theory – Wilber*

Ken Wilber's approach to understanding complex systems has been applied to numerous fields including medicine, leadership, politics, spirituality, and education. His integral framework draws on research insights from some of the world's greatest knowledge traditions. *The Shadow* was inspired by Wilber's insights and is indicative of the profundity of his work.

Wilber, K. (2000). *Integral Psychology: Consciousness, Spirit, Psychology, Therapy.* Boston, MA: Shambhala.

✿ *Creativity – Aitken*

In his book, *Zen Master Raven,* Robert Aitken explores the human experience through a series of counter-intuitive and provocative anecdotes. Based on unsolvable riddles, or Koans, Aitken challenges readers to explore their mental frameworks and expand them. Although not apparent from the title, this is a challenging read. *Mistakes* and *Inquiry* were inspired by Aitken's work.

Aitken, R. (2002). *Zen Master Raven: Sayings and Doings of a Wise Bird.* Boston, MA. Tuttle.

A Journey Into Culture

⚛ *Reframing Organizations – Bolman and Deal*

In their book *Reframing Organizations: Artistry, Choice and Leadership,* Lee Bolman and Terrence Deal take readers on a journey challenging the perception of organizational activity. They emphasize the artistry of leadership by considering situations from four different perspectives or frames. With the Structural Frame, they illustrate that how we are organized significantly impacts how we are. Through the Human Resource Frame, Bolman and Deal have us focus on the relationships between an organization and its people. With the Political Frame, they have us view organizations as political ecosystems replete with networks, agendas, negotiations, and coalitions. Finally, through the Symbolic Frame, we are exposed to the meaning imbedded in organizational culture and how culture plays a critical role in influencing behavior. Throughout this reframing approach, we extract different meaning from the same situations, thereby exposing the artistry of leadership as an inexact endeavor that allows for subtlety, ambiguity, and interpretation.

Bolman, L.G. & Deal, T.E. (2008). *Reframing Organizations: Artistry, Choice, and Leadership.* Hoboken, NJ: Wiley.

⚛ *Culture – Schein*

Edgar Schein in his seminal book *Organizational Culture and Leadership* illustrates the importance of understanding organizational culture and argues culture is the single most important source of information and understanding in our organizational existence. Schein asserts that *"organizational culture is to a group what personality or character is to an individual."* While an individual cannot hope to be effective in a social context without understanding people, leaders cannot hope to be effective in an organizational context without understanding culture. Schein portrays culture as an abstraction similar to personality, and like personality it has powerful behavioral and attitudinal consequences. Finally, Schein's ideas on culture and leadership complement Bolman and Deal's ideas on reframing organizations. Between these two perspectives the notion of the artistry in leadership begins to emerge.

Schein, E.H. (2004). *Organizational Culture and Leadership*. San Francisco, CA.:Jossey-Bass.

A Journey Into Control

❧ *Chaos – Wheatley*

Meg Wheatley introduced us to the power of chaotic behavior in the domain of leadership and organizations. She discussed how people in organizations pursue their own individual purposes while simultaneously working with one another towards a shared organizational purpose. To predict the individual behavior of any one person is impossible, or at least so it would seem. But if one were to "zoom out" and take a more macro view of an organization, the seemingly chaotic behavior at the individual level translates into recognizable and predictable patterns at a higher level.

Wheatley, M.J. (1994). *Leadership and the New Science: Learning About Organization from an Orderly Universe*. San Francisco, CA.: Berrett-Koehler.

A Journey Into Understanding

❧ *Relationships – Hinde*

Robert Hinde explored the complexity of a phenomenon we often take for granted: a relationship. He suggested this seemingly simple construct was actually a very complex and powerful force affecting our behavior. He argues a relationship is based on a series of interactions. These interaction are not only affected by previous interactions, but also attract expectations of future interactions as well. He proposed that relationships were more than the sum of interactions between participants, but were rather the combination of external forces, patterns, subjectivity, and context. In particular,

Hinde illuminated for us the linkages between relationships and power, trust, and context.

Hinde, R. A. (1980). *Towards Understanding Relationships*. Oxford, England: Academic Press.

⚘ *Sensemaking – Weick*

Karl Weick has profoundly influenced the way we think about thinking. For most of us, the lack of solitude and deep reflection in our lives has resulted in a lack of rigor in how we make sense. We rely on biases, attitudes, past experiences, and other people to help us as we process and respond to stimuli. We are usually unaware that we are engaged in this process of making sense of our social surroundings. He argues "making sense" is a fundamentally social process. Even when we make sense of things without the physical presence of others, our perceptions of their opinions and attitudes influence what we think. That being said, we still make sense in solitude differently than we do in the presence of others. Not only do we make sense differently, we make a different sense. When making sense in solitude we are alone in our perceptions, we make new sense based on our experiences and past sense. At this level of making sense we are more vulnerable to our own fears and biases than we would be in the presence of another.

Weick, K.E. (1995). *Sensemaking in Organizations*. Thousand Oaks, CA. Sage.

Other Great Works

We also feel compelled to share with you some other great works that have profoundly influenced our thinking. Although they don't necessarily fit into themes of this book as we have written it, anyone interested in continuing their deep-thinking journey should consider reading these exceptional works. Some of these books have won Pulitzer Prizes, a couple authors are Nobel Laureates and we even included an Oscar-winning film documentary. We hope you find these brilliant works as stimulating and inspiring as we have.

🖙 *Management of the Absurd – Richard Farson and Michael Crichton.* A provocative and counter-intuitive take on management. ISBN: 0684830442

🖙 *Big Mind, Big Heart – Dennis Merzel.* A fascinating journey into the human psyche. ISBN: 0977142337

🖙 *Political Savvy – Joel DeLuca.* A practitioner's guide to organizational politics. ISBN: 0966763602

🖙 *Influence – Robert Cialdini.* The leading authority on the under-pinnings of influence and persuasion. ISBN: 006124189X

🖙 *The Fifth Discipline – Peter Senge.* A revolutionary masterpiece that brought the systems approach to management and organizational learning. ISBN: 0385517254

🖙 *Social Cognition – Susan Fiske and Shelley Taylor.* Although a tough read, this book is a fascinating exploration of how we think together. ISBN: 0071284869

🖙 *Steps to an Ecology of Mind – Gregory Bateson.* In this classic work, Bateson presents an anthology of works across the fields of anthropology, psychiatry, epistemology and evolution examining the parameters, bounds and capabilities of human ability to learn. ISBN: 0226039056

🖙 *Handbook of Creativity – Robert Sternburg.* In an anthology of essays, Sternburg compiles many excellent essays and leading research on the evolution and emergence of creativity. ISBN: 0521572851

🖙 *Gödel, Escher, Bach – Douglas Hofstadter.* A Pulitzer Prize-winning masterpiece that explores patterns evident in mathematics, music and art and so much more. A difficult, immensely creative and revolutionary book. ISBN: 0465026567

☞ *Atlas Shrugged – Ayn Rand.* Regarded by many as one of the most influential books of the 20th century. In this fictional tale, Rand pits Socialism against Capitalism where she develops her philosophical theory of Scientific Objectivism around the most critical of all resources: innovation and the minds of people who create value for society. ISBN: 0452011876

☞ *Guns, Germs and Steel – Jared Diamond.* A Pulitzer Prize winning book that explores environmental factors that led to the development of Western societies and provides a compelling argument for economic determinism based on unlikely factors such as geographical distribution of large-seeded grasses and domesticatable mammals. ISBN: 0393061310

☞ *Micromotives and Macrobehavior – Thomas Schelling.* An early work of a Nobel Laureate in economics and one of the first books of its kind to reveal some of the more surprising properties of human behavior in economic systems. ISBN: 0393329461

☞ *Choices, Values and Frames – Daniel Kahneman and Amos Tversky.* This book includes some of the earliest theoretical and experimental work of Nobel Prize winner Danny Kahneman and his late co-author which led to the development of a field in psychology known today as *judgment and decision-making.* ISBN: 0521627494

☞ *Classic Writings on Management – Russell Ackoff.* Written by one of the most influential academics who was instrumental in developing what is commonly regarded today as "systems thinking." For someone who is interested in a first-book on systems thinking, this is it. ISBN: 0471316342

☞ *Models of Thought – Herbert Simon.* This compendium of works by Noble Laureate Herb Simon covers several decades of research on human cognition backed by extensive experimental research. Although a rather dense and difficult read, it is well worth the effort. ISBN: 0300024320

☞ *Systems Thinking, Systems Practice – Peter Checkland.* Checkland was one of the first to bring the concepts of systems engineering to management by emphasizing real-world practice. His ideas are near-revolutionary in terms of problem-solving. ISBN: 0471986062

☞ *How to Win Friends and Influence People – Dale Carnegie.* Arguably the most influential book written about influence, which by itself is quite a testament. Written in 1937, Carnegie's basic principles are still useful today for anyone who is interested in an easy read about the basics of human interaction. ISBN: 0671027034

☞ *Team of Rivals – Doris Kearns Goodwin.* Although this book is an historical account of Abraham Lincoln's 1860 bid for the U.S. presidency and his decision to add three of his opponents to his cabinet, it speaks volumes for how leaders should seek out critics and disconfirming evidence for their own beliefs when the stakes are high. ISBN: 0743270754

☞ *Wealth of Nations – Adam Smith.* Written in 1776, this masterpiece was one of the first works to start exploring the systemic interactions between human beings engaged in trade with one another. It's the foundational work of modern capitalism. ISBN: 0553585975

☞ *Thinking Strategically – Avinash Dixit and Barry Nalebuff.* A fun, light and easy read illustrating the necessity and power of thinking ahead and the importance of considering the actions of others before making decisions ourselves. ISBN: 0393310353

☞ *Freakonomics – Steven Levitt and Stephen J. Dubner.* Written by one of today's most prominent economists, this best-selling book advances many provocative hypotheses that emerged by asking nonobvious questions about issues that had previously been regarded as noncontroversial. ISBN: 0061234001

☞ *John von Neumann – Norman Macrae.* A biography written about one of the most notable and brilliant mathematicians who lived during the 20th century. As the "Albert Einstein" of mathematics, von Neuman's influence on the modern computer, the development of the first atomic bomb and his political views are unparalleled. ISBN: 0679413081

☞ *The Goal – Eliyahu Goldratt and Jeff Cox.* Selling more than two million copies, this books helped reshaped the way we think about the best-business practices by introducing us to the Theory of Constraints. ISBN: 0884270610

☞ *Fog of War – An Errol Morris film.* Although this is the only film on the list, it is an Academy Award winning documentary of an interview with former Secretary of Defense, Robert S. McNamara reflecting over his life experiences as a case study in leadership and learning. A book by the same title edited by James Blight and Janet Lang who served as academic advisors on the film contains the background source information. ISBN: 0742542211

☞ *Pearls for Breakfast – Gene Weingarten.* A Pulitzer Prize winning newspaper article reporting on a field experiment which illustrates all too well how our daily routines constrain us from "seeing" greatness. Appeared in the Sunday edition of the *Washington Post* on April 8, 2007, page W10.

APPENDIX B

The List

Although we promised a book without lists, we couldn't resist.

1. Compensation
2. Communication
3. Turnover
4. Office space
5. Career path
6. Parking
7. Budget
8. Advancement
9. Recognition
10. Leadership

To understand the significance of this list, visit

www.the52ndfloor.com

You can also join the following social networking groups:

Facebook: *The 52nd Floor*

LinkedIn: *Do You Have An Office On The 52nd Floor?*

APPENDIX C

Leadership Circles

We hope you've enjoyed your journey into leadership with *The 52nd Floor*. If you are like our clients and students, you might be wondering now, "What's next?" Well, because we believe a deep understanding of leadership emerges from inquiry and dialogue, we encourage you to continue on by sharing your questions, experiences and passion with others. Specifically, we suggest you start with what we call a *Leadership Circle*. A Leadership Circle is simply a gathering of people committed to exploring and reflecting deeply on leadership in a group environment. By starting with some of the stories in the book, you can use them to stimulate discussions with like-minded people in your organization or community. Since each of the stories is open to interpretation and has many levels, it is highly likely any group will come up with insights that you've never thought of before. More importantly, you'll get other people thinking deeply about leadership and how to make your own organization better.

Establishing a Leadership Circle for your organization or community is easy. All that is required is the following:

1. A commitment to thinking deeply and conversing openly about leadership with others.

2. A group of (4-20) like-minded people willing to participate.

3. Some stories from the book to get conversations started.

4. A place to meet for an hour or so once or twice a month.

For more information, please visit *www.leadershipcircles.org*

NOTES

A Journey Into Leadership

[1]Hobbes, T. (1947). *Hobbes's Leviathan: Reprinted from the Edition of 1651.* New York: Clarendon Press.

A Journey Into Human Nature

[1]Smith, A. (1776). *The Wealth of Nations.*

[2]Keynes, J.M. (1936). *General Theory of Employment Interest and Money.* London: MacMillan.

[3]Shaw, G.B. (1929). *Man and Superman, The Revolutionist's Handbook and Maxims for Revolutionists.* London: Constable.

[4]Skinner, B. (1965). *Science and Human Behavior.* New York: Free Press.

[5]Kahneman, D., Slovic, P. and Tversky, A. (1982). *Judgment Under Uncertainty: Heuristics and Bias.* Cambridge, UK: Cambridge University Press.

[6]Milgram, S. (1963). Behavioral study of obedience. *Journal of Abnormal and Social Psychology, 67,* 371–37.

[7]Maslow, A.H. (1943). Theory of human motivation, *Psychological Review, 50,* 370-96.

[8]Thanks to executive coach, Jim Selman, for this insight. See *http://www.paracomm.com.*

A Journey Into Culture

[1]Bolman, L.G., and Deal, T.E. (2003). *Reframing Organizations: Artistry, Choice, and Leadership.* San Francisco, CA: Jossey-Bass.

[2]Haney, C., Banks, C. and Zimbardo, P.G. (1972). Interpersonal Dynamics in a Simulated Prison, Technical report, Stanford University, Department of Psychology.

[3]Bongard, M. (1970). *Pattern Recognition.* New York: Spartan Books.

[4]Herrnstein, R. (1997). *The Matching Law: Papers in Psychology and Economics,"* Rachlin, H. and Laibson, D.I. (Eds). Boston, MA: Harvard Press.

[5]Foundalis, H.E. (2006). *Phaeaco: A Cognitive Architecture Inspired by Bongard's Problems.* Doctoral dissertation, Indiana University, Center for Research on Concepts and Cognition, Bloomington, Indiana.

[6]Langer, E.J. (1989). Mindfulness. Reading, MA. Addison-Wesley.

A Journey Into Control

[1]Barnsley, M. (1988). *Fractals Everywhere.* New York: Academic Press.

[2]Sierpiński Triangle generated with Java.

[3]Lorenz, E. (1996). *The Essence of Chaos.* University of Washington Press.

[4]Gleick, J. (1988). *Chaos: Making a New Science.* New York: Penguin Books.

[5]Wheatley, M. J. (1992). *Leadership and the New Science.* San Francisco: Berrett-Koehler Publishers.

[6]Hofstadter, D.R. (1980). *Godel, Escher, Bach: An Eternal Golden Braid.* New York: Basic Books.

[7]Autry, J.A. (1992). *Love and Profit: The Art of Caring Leadership.* New York: Harper Paperbacks.

[8]Davis, K.J. (1998). *IT Outsourcing Relationships: An Exploratory Study of Interorganizational Control Mechanisms,* Unpublished doctoral dissertation, Harvard University Graduate School of Business Administration.

The Journey's End

[1]Heskett, J. (2008). Why don't managers think deeply? *Working Knowledge,* Boston, MA: Harvard Business School. *http://hbswk.hbs.edu/cgi-bin/print?id=5952*

INDEX

ABOUT THE AUTHORS

 **DAVE LEVY** is an Associate Professor of Management at the United States Air Force Academy and holds a Ph.D. in Organizational Behavior from Cornell University. He served on active-duty with the Air Force and later worked as an organizational change consultant for both KPMG and Grant Thornton. He is a renowned speaker in the field of adaptive leadership.

 **JIM PARCO** is a Professor of Leadership and Strategy at Air Command and Staff College. He has served on the National Security Council at the White House and with the American Embassy in Tel Aviv. He holds an MBA from the College of William and Mary and a Ph.D. from the University of Arizona. He is widely published in the fields of game theory & decision-making.

 **FRED BLASS** is a faculty member in the College of Business and the Director of the Entrepreneurship Bootcamp for Veterans with Disabilities Program at Florida State University. His professional education includes a Ph.D. in Business Administration from Florida State University and a M.A. from George Washington University.

All three authors are Managing Principals of the RSC Consulting Group. For more information, please visit
www.rscgroup.org